MORE THAN A BUSINESS

The Amway enterprise is more than a business. It is an experience and a way of life unique in modern America. Controversial, fascinating and undeniably compelling, it has captured the interest of millions.

Now Charles Paul Conn, an award winning writer and author of two previous books about the Amway story, reveals the secrets behind the success of this phenomenal company.

AN UNCOMMON FREEDOM

Berkley Books by Charles Paul Conn

AN UNCOMMON FREEDOM
BELIEVE! (with Richard M. DeVos)
FATHERCARE
KATHY (with Barbara Miller)
MAKING IT HAPPEN
NO EASY GAME (with Terry Bradshaw)
THE POSSIBLE DREAM
PROMISES TO KEEP: THE AMWAY PHENOMENON
AND HOW IT WORKS
THE WINNER'S CIRCLE

About the Author

Charles Paul Conn is a veteran free-lance writer who has written books about football, politics, entertainment, religion, and the business world. He holds a Ph.D. degree in psychology from Emory University in Atlanta, Georgia. He currently teaches at Lee College in Cleveland, Tennessee, having completed a visiting fellowship at Harvard University. In addition to *The Possible Dream* — the book that catapulted to the top of national bestseller lists almost as soon as it was released — Conn has also written *Believe!* (with Richard M. DeVos), *No Easy Game* (with Terry Bradshaw), *The New Johnny Cash, Julian Carroll of Kentucky, Kathy* and *The Winner's Circle.*

An Uncommon Freedom

CHARLES PAUL CONN

BERKLEY BOOKS, NEW YORK

This Berkley book contains the complete
text of the original hardcover edition.
It has been completely reset in a typeface
designed for easy reading and was printed
from new film.

AN UNCOMMON FREEDOM

A Berkley Book / published by arrangement with
Fleming H. Revell Company

PRINTING HISTORY
Fleming H. Revell edition published 1982
Berkley edition / May 1983

ISBN: 0-425-08896-0

A BERKLEY BOOK ® TM 757,375
Berkley Books are published by The Berkley Publishing Group,
200 Madison Avenue, New York, New York 10016.
The name "BERKLEY" and the "B" logo
are trademarks belonging to Berkley Publishing Corporation.

PRINTED IN THE UNITED STATES OF AMERICA

20   19   18   17   16   15

To the memory of
PAUL DANA WALKER
my student, my friend,
and an uncommon person.

And to his parents,
PAUL and CARMELITA,
who have shown me that courage
is, indeed, grace under pressure.

Contents

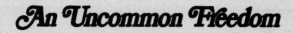

An Uncommon Freedom

1 An Uncommon Freedom

FREEDOM! It is mankind's most persistent dream.

For thousands of years, men and women have chased the dream of freedom. They have sought it, bought it, fought to gain it, and even died to preserve it. To be free has always been the great glittering goal of human history.

In this generation, the age-old dream of freedom is a reality for more men and women around the globe than ever before. Particularly in the great democracies of the United States and Canada, in England and Europe, and in the countries of the Western Pacific, individual freedoms are protected by the full force of law and government. "It's a free country!" Americans declare about their nation, and that claim is proudly made in dozens of other lands as well.

Certain personal freedoms are guaranteed to every citizen in any enlightened nation. These are the freedoms of speech, worship, the press, the freedom of movement, the freedom to vote, to assemble peaceably—the common freedoms of a democratic society. These rights are automatically granted, at birth, to every man and woman in a free land. They need not be earned; no price is paid for them; they are the legacy of those who, in generations past, have built and preserved the nation.

But these common freedoms, by themselves, do not make an individual fully liberated. There is another set of freedoms, rare and uncommon freedoms, that only a few individuals enjoy. These are the freedom *to be* what one wishes to be, to live where one wishes to live, to support the causes one believes in, to explore the full and exciting range of one's potential. Not many people ever experience that kind of freedom. It is a rare, uncommon freedom that must be won; it must be earned; it is the result of one's own individual effort and vision. This kind of freedom cannot be produced by an act of legislation. It cannot be granted by government decree. Uncommon freedom issues from uncommon achievement.

True liberty requires not just the political *right* to pursue happiness, but the material *means* to do so. A man may be free to eat, but unless he has food, that freedom is meaningless. He may have the *right* to live wherever he wishes, but only the money to buy the house he chooses will make him truly free to do so. A man is politically free to travel at will from New York to Seattle, but that freedom is meaningful only if he has the money and the time to take the trip.

The freedom of worship is a common freedom that can be guaranteed by the state; the freedom to give a million dollars to one's church is an uncommon freedom that can be enjoyed only by those people with a million dollars to give. The freedom to travel is common; the freedom to travel in one's own plane, on one's own schedule, is uncommon. The right to have a job is a common freedom; the liberty to work at what one most enjoys, without regard for the income, is an uncommon freedom.

Tens of millions of Americans, though politically free, are functionally not at all free to pursue life as they dream of it. They are free by law, but bound by the realities of no time, no money, and no prospect of things ever changing very much. There is, however, a particular group of business people who speak often of freedom, who say that they have found a new freedom in something they call "the Amway experience." When they talk of gaining their freedom in the "world of Amway," it is not the common political freedoms to which they refer, but the uncommon freedom to follow their dreams, the freedom to live uncommon lives.

Joe and Mary Logan have a transatlantic lifestyle. He is an American engineer who once worked at NASA in Houston, Texas; she is thoroughly British, with both her family and her citizenship in the United Kingdom. So they live both places. They own one home in Walnut Creek, California, and one in Birmingham, England, and travel between the two as the need or the inclination arises.

The freedom to maintain homes and family ties in separate countries, 7,000 miles apart, is a rare one, and it is financed not by Joe's engineering job—he left that years ago—but by the Logans' involvement in an Amway distributorship. The Logans are leaders in the Amway business, on both sides of the Atlantic; in each country they have used their extraordinary skills to develop large, profitable businesses. It is very unlikely that they could enjoy such a life through Joe's position as a salaried engineer. The governments of the United States and England can only give Joe and Mary Logan passports and the freedom to travel. It took the Amway business and their own adventuresome spirits to make their remarkable cross-cultural experience possible.

Jim and Sharon Janz, a personable young couple in British Columbia, are among the most influential people in Western Canada. Their support of various religious and political causes has a powerful impact far beyond their hometown of Vancouver. They have substantial financial resources and a virtually unlimited reservoir of personal energy and influence to lend to the conservative causes in which they believe.

The Janzes were not born with clout; they acquired it. Originally from small towns in Alberta, they rose to wealth and prominence in Canadian affairs by virtue of their success in the Amway business. It was as an Amway distributor that Jim Janz matured from an unknown schoolteacher into the poised and persuasive leader he is today. He is known and admired by hundreds of thousands of people across Canada and the United States and serves on the boards of some of his country's most important foundations.

The freedom Janz enjoys, to support so powerfully the values in which he believes, is an uncommon freedom that the state cannot give a man. It must be gained, and the structure through which he gained it has been the success of his Amway business.

Skip and Susan Ross love children, as most young parents do. They have definite opinions about what children should be taught, the attitudes they should develop, the influences to which they should be exposed. Most parents have such opinions.

But the Rosses are doing something about it. They operate a summer camp for children, a camp they founded, on land that they own. The camp is not merely a glorified baby-sitting service: it is a carefully planned environment designed to help kids develop healthy self-concepts, faith in themselves and other people, and positive outlooks on life. Nor is it a kind of emotional boot camp: the routine features first-rate programs in sports and horsemanship, and Ross uses his own considerable talent as a performer and entertainer to provide an atmosphere that is never dull.

Skip and Susan Ross have the resources to mount such an ambitious program and the savvy to make it successful, largely as a result of many years in the Amway business. Their investment capital, the pool of prospective campers, and the management experience gained in running one of Amway's largest distributorships have all combined naturally to make the Circle A Ranch possible.

It is a common thing to have strong opinions about kids these days, but quite rare to have the wherewithal to do something about it. Skip and Susan Ross have that uncommon freedom.

2 The Amway Experience

WHAT IS "the Amway experience"?

Amway Corporation is a company that makes and sells household products. The company is based in Michigan, but its products are sold in all fifty states of the United States and in twenty-four other countries. These products are not sold in stores, however, but by independent distributors who own their own businesses and sell products to friends and acquaintances.

But there is much more to the Amway experience than merely signing up as a distributor and selling the products. In addition to the sales activity itself, Amway distributors recruit other people to become distributors; and when they do, they share in both the work and the profits of getting that new distributor started. Strong ties form among these Amway distributors as they share the process of building a small business into what can potentially become a full-time career with a six-figure income. Sometimes an unusual camaraderie develops and a mystique attaches to the entire experience.

To understand why so many men and women in North America and elsewhere are becoming Amway distributors and why the experience so often becomes an important part of their lives, one must begin with Amway Corporation itself, and the two men who gave it birth.

Richard M. DeVos and Jay Van Andel were young boys who became friends while in high school in the early 1940s in Grand Rapids, Michigan. Both were bright and ambitious, both of Dutch ancestry, both from families oriented toward business. After high school graduation and military service during World War II, they returned to Grand Rapids, resumed their contact with one another, and started a small business together, a flying school called Wolverine Air Service.

That flying school was the first of many joint ventures, and elements of the Van Andel-DeVos pattern were evident even at that early stage. There was their entrepreneurial flair: neither man was himself a pilot, so they hired pilots and focused their energies on the marketing and management duties. There was their talent for improvisation: when the landing strip they used was flooded, they put pontoons on their planes and used the river for a "runway." And there was their ability to work smoothly as a team: what began as a rather ordinary friendship became a partnership that, more than thirty years later, is still a model of teamwork between two richly talented individuals joined in a single cause.

The Wolverine Flying Service was followed by several other business ventures in the late 1940s and early 1950s. There were winners, losers, and in-betweeners. Through the next few years, as DeVos and Van Andel honed their business skills, individually and as a partnership, they came to regard direct sales as the marketing wave of the future. They became distributors for Nutrilite, a California-based company that sold vitamins and food supplements, and found their own style as a partnership particularly well suited to the demands of direct selling. In 1959, when Nutrilite began to falter, victimized by internal disarray and a too-narrow product line, Van Andel and DeVos relinquished their distributorship in that company, turned their attention from food supplements to cleaning products, and organized a new company that they called Amway.

That was in 1959. They lived near the village of Ada, on the outskirts of Grand Rapids, and had built homes there. It was from the basement of their homes, with the help of their wives, Betty Van Andel and Helen DeVos, that they operated the new company. After a year they acquired property in Ada, a tiny forty-by-sixty-foot building that had been a service station. They began looking for new products—high-quality cleaning products that were good enough to sell easily and to create repeat customers for their distributors. It was an unremarkable beginning, and if it had failed, would have been no different from the stories of thousands of other small-time business-men in America who have tried to make it on their own. But the new venture called Amway succeeded spectacularly, almost from the very beginning, and has become one of the legendary stories in Ameri-can business history.

Twenty-four years later, Amway Corporation is the second-largest direct sales company in the world. One million distributors now are part of its "family," in every nook and cranny of America and in eleven foreign countries. They distribute over 300 products, most of which are manufac-tured by Amway itself. In fiscal 1981, Amway's corporate revenues were $1.1 billion, with esti-mated retail sales by Amway distributors of $1.4 billion. The corporation employs 7,000 people to manufacture the products and provide service for the distributor force, operating from corporate facilities around the world which occupy over 6 million square feet of floor space.

The corporate giant that Amway has become is still headquartered in Ada and is still personally led by Van Andel and DeVos, who own the com-pany and serve as chairman of the board and presi-dent, respectively.

But corporate statistics alone cannot tell the story of the enormous vitality and energy that flow through the Amway system. In a period of eco-nomic uncertainty, Amway is one case of a robust and thriving company that has been unaffected by any of the recent national recessions. It has grown in the last four years in giant leaps: $500 million in 1978; $800 million the next year; $1.1 billion in 1980; and $1.4 billion in 1981. Growth in markets outside North America has been even more dramatic, exceeding 100 percent in many countries, in the 1981 fiscal year.

Business is so good that the corporation works literally around the clock to keep with the pace set by its distributors. In April of 1981, a new research-and-development building was opened, with 24 research labs for testing and developing new products. Former President Gerald R. Ford, a longtime friend of Amway, gave the dedication address. A huge fleet of tractor-trailer rigs, each of them hauling 22 tons of products, shuttles between the Ada plant and Amway warehouses across the country. The company's printing presses churn out millions of pieces of promotional and product literature for distributor use. A staff of 26 attorneys handle Amway's legal affairs; nearly 2 dozen pilots and ground personnel keep its air fleet flying; 270 research-and-development employees review 3,000 new product ideas annually.

At Amway, come inflation or recession or whatever, business is booming in every area of the company's operation.

The fuel that keeps the Amway machinery moving is the energy of those 1 million distributors. Their stories are best told in their own words; but, first, here are a few vocabulary notes to help in understanding them.

Large distributorships are built not only by selling products, but by recruiting other people into the business. This recruiting effort is called "sponsoring," and being sponsored by someone already involved is the only way for a new person to join the Amway sales force. When distributors sponsor someone new, they assume the task of training that new distributor and helping him or her succeed.

The typical method of introducing prospective distributors to Amway is by explaining the company's sales and marketing plan, called simply "the Plan" in Amway jargon. This is sometimes done by use of a diagram in which distributorships are symbolized by circles, and thus "showing the circles" or "drawing the circles" is another way Amway people often describe the sponsoring process. Amway Corporation gives awards to distributors whose overall sales-and-sponsoring activity reaches certain levels. In a kind of in-group shorthand, Amway people use these award designations to identify the size and success of a person's business—almost as a rank of importance, much as military rank is used. The sequence of these ranks gives a rough idea of the relative level of income and importance they describe. The first rank is that of Direct Distributor, which is the point at which the Amway person is making about $1,000 a month gross profit. Reaching that first award level is spoken of as "breaking Direct" or "going Direct." After that, the award levels go up to

Ruby, Pearl, Emerald, then Diamond.

The Diamond level represents a major achievement in Amway, an income in the neighborhood of $75,000 a year and informal leadership of several hundred other distributors. A business that is twice as large as that required for Diamond status is a Double Diamond award; then up to Triple Diamond; followed by the level of Crown Direct; and finally the top rank in the world of Amway, that of Crown Ambassador.

Distributors reaching these levels receive more than applause for their efforts. Cash bonuses are paid every year for maintaining various levels. In 1980, for example, the largest Emerald bonus was $102,000; the top Diamond bonus was $150,000; the largest Double Diamond bonus was $173,000. All these are one-time, lump-sum bonuses that vary in size from year to year and that are contingent upon individual performance. But the idea is that Amway's top producers receive more for their efforts than baubles and bangles; the recognition and lapel pins Amway gives are backed up by solid monetary rewards.

The more symbolic rewards are also important to Amway distributors, however. Chief among them are expense-paid trips, beginning with one to Ada for a three-day seminar when the distributor "goes Direct." Reaching Diamond status brings an invitation to join Diamond Club, with expense-paid seminars in the Virgin Islands, seminars on one of the Amway yachts, and annual seminars in such resort areas as Hawaii. The most elite club in

Amway is the Executive Diamond Council; membership in that group entitles a distributor to first-class seminar trips to the group's annual meetings in exotic destinations: Switzerland; Rio de Janeiro; the Riviera; and Dubrovnik, Yugoslavia, in recent years.

One of the most prized rewards in Amway occurs when the rank of Double Diamond is reached. At that time, a day is set aside in honor of the distributor, and Amway employees throughout the Ada facility wear lapel badges proclaiming it to be, for example, JARRETT DAY, to celebrate the Double Diamond status of Jerry and Cheri Jarrett from California. The entire family is flown to Ada for a VIP tour on their day, with one of Amway's jets flying the family on one leg of the trip. This particular reward is one that the distributor's entire group can enjoy, and it is regarded by many people as the single most memorable experience on the path from Direct to Crown Ambassador.

The experience of the Jarretts, in fact, illustrates well the importance of corporate gestures like these to the distributor force. Jerry Jarrett was an orthopedic surgeon in California; Cheri was a high-school physical-education teacher and former stewardess, who grew increasingly weary of working while she mothered her young children. When she and Jerry saw the Amway business, they had a five-month-old child, and she was interested in Amway as a means of earning income without leaving her baby to go off to work.

What began as Cheri's business became a joint

effort, and Jerry eventually saw it as a way to augment, or even replace, his own income as a physician. So they built their distributorship to Diamond level, then to Double Diamond, and the word came from Amway that August 7, 1981, had been designated as Jarrett Day at Ada. The Jarretts' group had bumper stickers printed that read, THE JET IS COMING AUGUST 7. They answered their phones by saying, "Hello, the jet is coming August seventh!" This was one reward that all the Jarretts' friends could enjoy with them.

When August 7 arrived, and the Amway BAC 1-11 flew into the Chico, California, airport, hundreds of enthusiastic distributors were there, creating an exuberant holiday mood, laughing and applauding, taking pictures, and waving proudly to the Jarrett family as they walked on board. It is a scene that captures the rare quality of the Amway experience. There is the success of the Jarretts, but even more so, the warm and happy send-off, the readiness of hundreds of Amway friends to enjoy their success with them. It was the kind of mood and the kind of moment that makes the Amway experience an uncommon one. "We are in this together," the crowd was saying. "You have achieved, and we are happy with you!" In this tough and competitive world, that is a rare and welcome message.

3 Growing Up

IN 1983, as Amway Corporation moves toward its twenty-fifth anniversary, the scope of the company's activities grow increasingly ambitious. Year after year of profitable and rapid growth have transformed Amway from a young, if promising, company into a force to be reckoned with in the American society.

Direct-sales companies have always had an image problem. The origins of direct-sales marketing go back to village peddlers, who trundled their wares through streets and neighborhoods, selling to passersby or to housewives at their doorsteps. Though most retailing has moved from the streets to stores, the practice of taking goods directly to the customer has persisted, often in the form of door-to-door salesmen who trudge through neighborhoods, indiscriminately ringing doorbells in search of customers.

Direct sales, in the modern era, is emphatically *not* a door-to-door approach. As it is practiced in Amway, direct sales means that distributors sell products to people they already know, developing a client list from relatives, friends, and neighbors. Amway distributors are discouraged from random soliciting, being urged to serve a few customers well, rather than approaching the marketplace peddler style. The theme in today's Amway is a "professional approach" to direct sales, emphasizing the long-term career potential of a well-managed distributorship. But the public perception that direct sales is door-to-door and that multilevel companies are unproven and perhaps unstable figures on the business landscape has persisted, requiring a corporation like Amway to work doubly hard to earn a national image of permanence and respectability.

Public acceptance of Amway's corporate maturity seems finally to have arrived. The company's robust financial position and its reputation for dealing generously with its distributors have come to be recognized and respected, first by the business community and now, in trickle-down fashion, by the public at large. Leading the way in Amway's relentless campaign for public appreciation are cofounders Van Andel and DeVos themselves. The acclaim that they have personally received as leaders in the business community has been the spearhead for the upgrading of Amway's image on a broader scale.

DeVos has been a board member of the National

Association of Manufacturers; is currently board chairman of Gospel Films, Inc.; and is a director of many local clubs and foundations. He served in 1981 as the cochairman of the committee to dedicate the new Gerald R. Ford Presidential Museum in Grand Rapids. Another activity that drew national attention to DeVos in 1981 was his innovative chairmanship of the National Republican Leadership Council, a group of influential businessmen that seeks to elect Republicans to Congress.

DeVos has of course received numerous service awards and honorary doctoral degrees over the years. In one example, he received *Industry Week's* Excellence in Management Award, winning the honor from among such finalists as the chairman of United States Steel Corporation and the chairman of Mobil Oil Corporation. In making the award, the prestigious magazine called DeVos "a businessman-philosopher who has mastered the art of communication."

Both Rich and Helen DeVos have been aggressive boosters of Grand Rapids civic projects, especially in the arts. A new, dazzling 2,500-seat arts center in downtown Grand Rapids is named DeVos Hall in their honor, and the *Grand Rapids Press* recently observed that "The Grand Rapids Symphony Orchestra has taken vast strides in quality on the strength of DeVos money. . . ."

Jay Van Andel has long been a shaker and mover in Republican party politics and was for several years finance chairman of the Michigan

Republican Party. He is the founding chairman of Citizen's Choice, a grass-roots lobbying group that seeks reduction in government spending and regulation. His wife Betty has been active in women's issues and serves on hospital, opera, and education boards.

Van Andel recently completed a term as national chairman of the United States Chamber of Commerce, a post that placed him squarely at the top of the American business community. He pursued the work of the chamber in a characteristically vigorous fashion, making speeches in some twenty-five cities and several foreign countries. He received massive publicity in his role as chamber head, almost all of it favorable. Newspapers used words such as "rousing," "hard-hitting," and "impassioned" to describe his speeches; and one national columnist wrote of a particular Van Andel address: "I wish I had power to put it into the hands of every member of the House and Senate."

The Amway board chairman's most recent major involvement was his chairmanship of the Netherlands-American Bicentennial Commission. In that role he led an office and staff in Washington, which directed the celebration of the two-hundredth anniversary of the signing of America's treaty of friendship with the Netherlands, and developed over one hundred sports, cultural, and business events, including two visits to the United States by Queen Beatrix of the Netherlands.

• •. •

In a variety of other ways, Amway Corporation is stretching its muscles. Its national television advertising, formerly confined to the network news shows, now includes occasional sponsorship of major coast-to-coast "specials" such as the Bob Hope Special in October of 1981 and sponsorship of "Hockey Night in Canada" on Canadian network TV.

The 1982 Tournament of Roses Parade included a gigantic float from Amway, a salute to Dutch-American friendship titled "Hands Across the Sea." Amway Diamonds Harm and Anne Berghuis, from the Netherlands, and Crown Ambassadors Dan and Bunny Williams, from the United States, rode the float to symbolize the 200-year tradition of cooperation between the two nations. The float received the "International Trophy" from Rose Bowl Parade officials.

In February of 1982, Amway sponsored a concert tour of seventeen European cities by Msitslav Rostropovich and the National Symphony Orchestra. Rostropovich, the world's most celebrated cellist, came to the United States from the Soviet Union in 1975, in a widely publicized defection. He visited Amway headquarters in Ada prior to his European tour, meeting Amway employees and playing in the Center of Free Enterprise as a gesture of thanks for Amway's largesse. His concert tour in February drew predictably heavy attention from the European press, and Amway distributors in the Netherlands, France, the United

Kingdom and West Germany were able to point to yet another indication of Amway's emergence as a major corporate presence in those countries.

In the United States, few developments have signaled Amway's growing maturity more forcibly than its purchase of Mutual Broadcasting System in 1978. Under Amway ownership, the radio network has grown to include 950 affiliated radio stations and in 1981 initiated use of a new $10 million satellite system. *Cash Box,* the trade journal of broadcasting, says Mutual has "sped to the forefront" of the industry with this new system of affiliate interconnections. Amway, through Mutual, now also owns two major big-city radio stations, WCFL in Chicago and WHN in New York City.

In 1981, Amway completed the first phase of a $64 million hotel project in downtown Grand Rapids. Purchasing the old and tattered Pantlind Hotel, a Grand Rapids landmark since 1902, Amway rebuilt it into a new world-class hotel called the Amway Grand Plaza. With an additional 28-floor tower building projected for completion in 1983, the Amway Grand Plaza will give Grand Rapids a new 700-room hotel facility, completing that city's downtown rebirth and solving Amway's chronic problem of providing hotel space for visitors to its Ada headquarters.

Amway had entered the hotel field earlier, purchasing the Peter Island Yacht Club and Resort in the British Virgin Islands. The 500-acre Peter Island resort was recently dubbed "one of the five most glamorous anchorages in the world" by *Motor Boating and Sailing* magazine.

But the Amway Grand Plaza catapulted the corporation into a new public visibility in the Grand Rapids area and elsewhere. The *Detroit Free Press* called the hotel project "the most visible symbol of Amway's increasing wealth and prominence," and various other newspapers around the country pointed to the hotel opening as evidence that Amway has firmly established itself as a mainstream corporate leader in the United States.

For anyone who still thinks of Amway as a quaint little soap company with a handful of door-to-door salesmen, this "new Amway," symbolized by its Grand Plaza Hotel, must be a startling revelation indeed. The hotel was formally opened in late 1981, a part of a week-long "Celebration on the Grand" which also included the dedication of the Ford Presidential Museum. That week of festivities served to underscore dramatically just how far Van Andel, DeVos, and Amway have come since 1959. As guests arrived at the hotel, so rarefied was the atmosphere, that mere governors and movie stars did not rate a personal, front-door greeting. An observer, standing inside the Amway Grand Plaza lobby, could watch as the DeVoses and Van Andels, relaxed and smiling, welcomed to *their* hotel President and Mrs. Ronald Reagan, Vice-President and Mrs. George Bush, Secretary of State Alexander Haig, President and Mrs. Gerald Ford, Lady Bird Johnson, Henry and Nancy Kissinger, President José Portillo of Mexico, and Prime Minister Pierre Trudeau of Canada, and former French head-of-state Giscard d'Estaing.

It is little wonder that the public awareness of Amway is growing and becoming more positive each year. Van Andel acknowledges that things are changing. "No question about it," he agrees. "Our efforts *are* paying off. We get different press coverage today; the aura is all different. That doesn't avoid the possibility of getting an occasional negative story in any given newspaper. Those things can always happen. But by and large the media have a different picture of Amway now."

4 The Home Team

PRESIDENT DEVOS, when asked how he and Van
Andel manage such a fast-growing company, once
remarked that "the larger Amway grows, the
easier our job becomes. We have a management
team that really runs this company on a day-to-day
basis, and they deserve much of the credit for the
smooth operation around here."

As Van Andel and DeVos are increasingly called
upon for duty in a wider arena, the workaday con-
cerns of operating their multi-national corporation
fall largely to a team of five executive vice-presidents. For such a young company, the second-level
Amway leaders are a veteran group; none has been
with the corporation less than twelve years.
Though all come from fairly traditional corporate
—rather than entrepreneurial—backgrounds, they
have been around Amway long enough to absorb
the style and spirit of the DeVos-Van Andel

"dream" and provide an effective in-house counterpoint to the Amway distributor force. They are the Home Team, and anyone who spends time with them can readily see that they are not mere hirelings; the pursuit of the Amway ideal belongs to them as surely as it does to Van Andel and DeVos or any distributor.

Though the cofounders vigorously resist any suggestion that there is a "first among equals" in the Home Team, the one executive veep who has been with them longest, indeed since before Amway itself began, is Bill Halliday. For fifteen years he was the private attorney for the Amway owners and in that role drafted, in 1959, the original documents of incorporation for the company. He signed on as chief legal counsel, in an official capacity, in 1966, and now is designated executive vice-president—corporate services.

Halliday is bright and intense; he was a member of Phi Beta Kappa as an undergraduate at the University of Michigan and received his law degree there. As a staff member of the judge advocate general's office of the United States Army during World War II, Halliday learned Japanese, interrogated Japanese prisoners of war, and returned home to western Michigan to serve as a prosecuting attorney in the immediate postwar years. He became a friend of Van Andel and DeVos in the early 1950s, when they came to him for a routine legal matter; and though a staff of attorneys now handle the company's affairs, he remains their chief counsel and the symbol of Amway's legal rectitude. He has been a national board member of the Better Business Bureau and has helped to forge the reputation of unimpeachable integrity that Amway enjoys today.

The executive vice-president who is perhaps most visible to the distributor force is Laurie Mulham, an Australian-born marketing whiz who serves as vice president in the area of world-wide sales. The nature of Mulham's job requires that he maintain a high profile to Amway distributors, and Mulham carries off that assignment with dash and aplomb. He somehow manages to combine excitement and sophistication in a singularly effective personal style that has made him a popular figure among distributors in the United States and abroad; they point to him as an exemplar of the "new Amway," forceful and enthusiastic without any loss of his cosmopolitan urbanity.

Mulham comes by this blend naturally; he has lived and worked in various parts of the world and is comfortable in virtually any culture. He joined Amway in 1971 to direct its expansion into Australia, the first of ten countries in which he has planted the Amway flag. His conversation still betrays those Australian origins—he still calls a colleague "mate" on occasion—but he is in every sense a citizen of the world. On a management team that tilts heavily toward home-grown Michiganders, he is perhaps the perfect member to lead the distributor force of a company that is so broadly based in fifty states and many nations.

Orville Hoxie, vice-president—operations, has been with Amway for sixteen years. He is responsible for manufacturing, an enormous task at a company that makes virtually all its products and prides itself on their competitiveness in the national marketplace. Hoxie's academic background (Notre Dame University and the University of Michigan) is in chemical and metallurgical engineering, and his corporate experience prior to coming to Amway was with General Motors and Bissell Corporation.

Another University of Michigan graduate is Gordon Teska, who serves as chairman of the company's marketing committee from his post as executive vice-president—marketing. Teska is the senior member of the Home Team in years of actual Amway service, having come to Ada in 1964 from the management services division of a large CPA firm. He is responsible for the corporation's research and development, quality control, and market research.

Rounding out the roster of executive vice-presidents is Robert Hunter, who as head of corporate development manages Amway's growing portfolio of subsidiary divisions. Principal among these are Mutual Broadcasting and Nutrilite Products. He has a graduate degree in physical chemistry from Penn State University. Though his current duties take him far afield from the soap and detergent industry, Hunter is the sole member of Amway's management team with a corporation background in that field; he came to Ada from the Colgate-Palmolive Company, where he was a research chemist.

For a privately held company such as Amway, with ownership and policy-making leadership still concentrated in the persons of Jay Van Andel and Rich DeVos, the quality of the Home Team is understandably an important point of reassurance for its hundreds of thousands of distributors. Both cofounders are still young and active chief executive officers and show no signs of losing their prodigious appetite for corporate leadership. They seem not to be sated by their own enormous personal success and speak convincingly of the challenge they find in putting Amway Corporation into the very top level of American businesses.

The matter of succession, of the person or persons to whom Amway leadership might eventually fall when the cofounders are no longer active, remains a subject of low-level speculation, but only that. Both DeVos and Van Andel have children who are pursuing management careers within the company, following a thorough leadership-training program to which they have taken with considerable aptitude. The cofounders acknowledge that the subject is one which they have quite naturally discussed, that contingency plans to provide for an emergency are in place, but otherwise decline to comment on the matter.

For now, it is enough that the Van Andel-DeVos partnership is working better than ever, with no hint that a withdrawal from their extraordinary personal leadership is in sight. Depending on a capable Home Team for the daily nuts-and-bolts management, Amway's cofounders are able to lead their company and still find time for the broader civic involvement that is creating a growing national appreciation for the Amway experience.

5 So Pro

ONE RESULT of this improving public image is a growing readiness of upper-income professionals to join the Amway distributor team.

The medical profession occupies what is perhaps the highest notch on the American status ladder. The median annual income for United States doctors is $74,000, highest among all occupational groups. But physicians are not immune to the pressures of America's economic erosion, nor to the frustrations of feeling trapped in a profession that sometimes demands more of them than they wish to give. "The better I did," one surgeon described it, "the worse off I was. My practice owned me. The more successful it became, the less I enjoyed it."

The career path of Lee Waters, M.D., illustrates the dilemma. Dr. Waters was a pediatrician with a thriving practice in the small upstate Michigan town of Petoskey. His wife, **Barb**, was active in civic affairs, and was serving a term as mayor of the town. It was she who first began to seek supplemental income that would relieve the pressure of Lee's demanding medical practice. "M.D.'s aren't allowed to quit until they die," Barb asserts. "I read an insurance-company report that the average M.D. dies at the age of fifty-six. I thought, *Not my husband!* I was determined we were going to find something different before he fell over in some clinic somewhere, someday!"

Lee Waters was on the job upwards of ninety hours weekly, was on call for a twenty-four-hour stretch at the pediatric clinic every four days, and was moonlighting at a hospital emergency room five nights a month. "He looked dreadful!" Barb says. "I thought he wasn't going to live to be fifty years old!" The Waterses looked for a solution in the stock market, then they tried real estate. No solutions there. "I like medicine," Lee explained, "but I was looking for something that would give me a little free time. Working at medicine so many hours each week gets a little tiresome sometimes."

The solution came from an unexpected source: a twenty-one-year-old mother who brought her baby into the Waters' pediatric office one afternoon. Nervously, but without intimidation, she told her doctor, "My husband and I would like to talk to you about something that changed my life." To her surprise, he agreed; and a few days later the young couple came to the Waterses' home to show them the Amway marketing plan.

The distributorship that began that night has become a Double Diamond business with an income larger than Lee Waters' medical practice had provided. He has now retired entirely from that practice, though he does volunteer medical work occasionally, as in a recent volunteer stint with children in Jamaica. After eighteen years as a physician, he says, much of his work had become routine, and he has rediscovered the sense of challenge in the pursuit of his goals in Amway.

Dr. Clayton Overton, an orthopedic surgeon in the Sacramento area, prefers to maintain his medical practice, though he and his wife Charlotte have built a Diamond business and have sponsored other physicians who, like Waters, have left medicine to go full-time. The Overtons are Tulane graduates from the Deep South, who settled in the foothill country of northern California several years ago.

They came into business in response to the soaring cost of malpractice insurance for California physicians. (Insurance costs had risen from $7,000 to $25,000 a year since they had been in California.) The Overtons are particularly successful in sponsoring other M.D.'s who have gone on to be Diamonds themselves, primarily in the Bay Area. These couples include one New Orleans husband-wife team who *both* practice medicine.

Clayton Overton's attitude toward the medical profession sounds much like that of Lee Waters: "I love medicine, but I want time for my family. I didn't see any way to do that with my practice as it was. I saw that an Amway income would give me a way to control my practice, rather than vice versa. Working sixty-plus hours a week gets old after a while, no matter how much you love it.''

Though the Watergate decade knocked a bit of the luster off the public image of attorneys in this country, there is still enough of the old Perry Mason glamour left to put the legal profession near the top of the heap in occupational status.

Jim Jones, a forty-two-year-old attorney from Tampa, Florida, is an example of a successful lawyer who has become an Amway leader in recent years. Jim and his wife, Julie, are a showcase example of the all-American couple. They have had a healthy slice of the good life: both are private pilots; they ski in Europe; their two daughters are models of adolescent charm; and they lived well for sixteen years on Jim's income as an attorney in private practice. But a cloud appeared on the horizon seven years ago: Florida legislators began revising the law on workman's compensation cases and other legal procedures involving personal-injury suits. This legal speciality area had comprised 90 percent of Jim's practice. Sweeping changes in those procedures would force a wholesale revision of his practice.

So Jim began looking for an alternative and found it in Amway. He and Julie are Diamonds; he has not practiced law for over two years, and they have a larger income today, with far greater freedom, than in his best years as an attorney. The unexpected bonus, according to the Joneses, has been that their work in Amway is more stimulating and interesting than the legal routine they left. "I was doing the same thing over and over," Jim says, "the same cases with different names. Practicing law really was no fun to me anymore. This business is a new challenge every day; there are many intangible benefits that I didn't anticipate when I first got in."

Another professional who looked down the road to where his career led and decided to seek a wider set of options was John Vaughan, a career military officer who retired from the United States Air Force at the rank of lieutenant colonel. Vaughan was a captain when he and Pat, his wife, joined the business. They were both in graduate school at the time—he to complete a Ph.D. in engineering; she, an M.Ed.

"I looked at Amway because I saw it as a chance to increase my options after the military," he explains. And it did. He retired in 1979 to the income of a Double Diamond; whereupon, with the thoroughness characteristic of a career military man, he sat down and wrote a letter to his sponsor "thanking him for saving me from twenty more years!"

6 Breaking Out

AMERICA—the Land of Opportunity. The place where an individual has always had an honest shot at the Big Time. However poor the start in life, there is an opportunity to break out to a richer life. That is the American Way, the tradition of hungry, hard-working men and women breaking out of the life of the have-nots, to take their places among the haves. That tradition has in recent years felt the squeeze of new, grim realities. The golden promise of the New World has receded a bit, and some argue that it is gone altogether—that for a person to begin with nothing and work his way into the ranks of the wealthy is virtually a thing of the past, a casualty of our times. People just don't have an honest chance to do that anymore, they say.

In Amway, the tradition of breaking out is still alive and well. For all the talk of doctors and lawyers coming into Amway, for all the stories of distributorships built with country-club connections, for all the long lists of Ph.D.'s and M.D.'s and upper-level types becoming Diamonds, the Amway experience is still very much what it always has been—an ideal vehicle for upward social mobility. You get in, and you work hard, and you make it to the top: that is the old-fashioned American Dream, the possibility of overcoming deficiencies with hard work, of making the quantum leap from where one is now to where one wants to be.

Fred and Linda Harteis have always believed in the American Dream and found in Amway a means of living it out. They are Double Diamonds in Pennsylvania and have achieved material success far beyond the previous generations in both their family backgrounds. The luxuries and comforts that they enjoy today were unimaginable to their parents and grandparents, and the Harteises are acutely aware of that. They have not forgotten from whence they came and seem genuinely humbled by the giant leap forward they have achieved. "I grew up on a farm, and I was taught how to work," Fred says. "I consider myself to be blessed in that I wasn't born with a silver spoon in my mouth. We never had much. I can remember putting cardboard inside my boots to keep my feet dry. But we knew how to work and how to take care of ourselves."

Fred had a farm boy's shyness as a teenager, but his competitive nature and mental toughness were

evident even at that age. He was told he was too
small (5' 8", 125 pounds) to play varsity football in
high school, but went out for the team anyway.
One hundred and twenty-five boys showed up the
first day of practice, to compete for forty-four
uniforms, and practically nobody gave him a
chance to wear one. But by the end of the season,
Too-Small Harteis had not only made the team,
but was a starting halfback. It was a major turning
point for him: "I hated losing, and I learned that I
didn't have to lose if I worked hard enough. My
goal was to start at halfback, and I was willing to
pay whatever price was necessary. Whatever it
took. I learned that you can have what you want in
life if you pay your dues."

It was a lesson that stayed with him. His determination to have what he wanted from life led him
to college. "I was told I needed a college degree to
'make it.' So I went. I didn't have any money, so I
worked to earn it."

Upon graduation, the young Harteis couple
moved to accept a teaching job at the local high
school. In his usual pattern, Fred was soon doing
more than a regular nine-to-five shift. Frustrated
by the modest life-style his teaching salary provided, he began working at a part-time job and
teaching night classes. His immediate goal was to
move from his seventy-five-dollar-a-month rented
house into a home of his own. During that time, he
heard about Amway.

"I had no idea it would be something big. I got

in strictly for enough money to have a home of my own—two hundred dollars a month, that's what I was after. Just two hundred dollars a month to buy a house for Linda.''

As for Linda, she was just as determined to get out of her little rented house, but she soon saw other potential payoffs from the business. When she and Fred attended their first weekend seminar, she was impressed with the visible way Amway couples seemed to care for each other. She saw strong marriages, and that got her attention. ''That first weekend, I saw so many men who seemed to really love their wives, I thought, *Wouldn't it be great if Fred felt that way about me?* At that time in our marriage, I was guessing. I suppose that was what hooked me into this business; I saw so much love and mutual respect between husband and wife. And, you know, that's exactly the way it has turned out for us. The most important thing we've received from this business is a love that we never had before in our marriage.''

The Harteis Amway experience was a successful one from the beginning, but along the way, they had to overcome some discouragement from skeptical friends and colleagues. ''I got a lot of free advice, especially from some of my fellow teachers, and all of it was negative. The main objection was simply that it wouldn't work, that I wouldn't be able to make any money at it.'' Even his father-in-law offered an opinion that Fred couldn't make it work. He backed up his prediction with a fifty-dollar bet, and Fred accepted the wager without a moment's hesitation.

Several months later, when Fred won that bet, he was not reluctant to ask for the fifty dollars. His father-in-law dutifully delivered the check, whereupon Fred tore it in half and handed it back. "I don't want your money," he said, smiling. "I just don't want you putting down my business. If I had listened to you, I wouldn't have even tried it!"

That would have been a tragedy. Fred and Linda Harteis were made for the Amway business as kangaroos were made for jumping. By the age of twenty-seven, Fred had retired from teaching and was a full-time Diamond; today they wear Double Diamond pins and are members of the elite Executive Diamond Council. "Amway has given us a whole new way of living that we couldn't have even conceived of as children," Linda says. "Our children have grown up in the business; they were babies when we started. They will never know anything else, and that makes it all worthwhile."

That is the essence of upward mobility. A couple who grow up with cardboard in their shoes pass on to their children every advantage that money can buy. "My mom was a great woman," Linda reflects. "She raised eight children all by herself. We didn't have much money, but we always had love. Plenty of love. I look at my mother, and I feel that she deserves so much more than she has ever received. Fred and I are seeing to it that she has lots of nice things now. I want my mom to know what the good life is like. She deserves it."

Those who know Fred and Linda Harteis do not doubt that mom will have it. As a result of their Amway income, they are in a position to afford just about whatever they choose to do. And that, after all, is a pretty good way of describing the American Dream.

The Harteis experience, in various forms, has been repeated many times during Amway's twenty-four-year history. Amway lore includes legitimate Horatio Alger stories, enough to fill a dozen books, of men and women who had the courage to break out to a better life.

There are Jim and Betty Jean Brooks from Washington state. Jim drove a logging truck only six years ago and describes himself as "a loser, a negative person who was unwilling to dream." They lived in an 1,100-square-foot home (including the garage) and had little prospect of doing better until they entered Amway. He attacked Amway as a hungry boy attacks a T-bone steak. He practiced showing the Plan with Betty Jean as a substitute prospect, calling her "Joe" or "Pete" to simulate the sponsoring situation. They are Diamonds today, he says, "Because I use common sense. I have to. I don't have a wall full of college degrees. I use common sense to build this business because it's all I have."

There is Pepper Purpera, a welder before Amway, who is now a Diamond in Louisiana. He admits that the thought of calling prospects "scared me to death" when he and wife, Deanna, began.

"I was petrified," he says. "I was willing to do almost anything to avoid making that call." But now he is a high-income businessman, not a wage-earning welder, and things have changed. He has greater confidence and with good reason: "People are listening better now. Fellows that wouldn't think about the business a few years ago are eager to get in now."

Or consider the case of Jake and Helen Funk. They were teenage sweethearts in Winnipeg, Manitoba. Jake grew up on a farm, one of nine children, and remembers his childhood as having more love than money. When he and Helen married, they were twenty years old and rather naive about life. "We had lots of dreams, but not much else."

They worked hard, saved their money, and seemed to be getting ahead financially, when Jake lost his management job. He finally found a new job, driving a fuel truck, but it paid too little to cover their monthly obligations, and the Funks dug a deeper hole for themselves. They were borrowing each month, merely to buy groceries and pay bills. They realized they needed backup income before their situation became hopeless.

The Funks had been shown the Amway business several years earlier. They sang in the Sacred Music Society, and a fellow singing bass beside Jake said "Come over after rehearsal; I've got a great idea I want to share with you." They got into Amway at that time, but had dropped out without building a business. Now, with the wolf howling loudly at the door of the Funk household, they decided to try it again. This time they took it seriously, and this time it worked. A rally in Winnipeg was the catalyst. The speakers were Frank and Rita Delisle. Frank was a former printer from California who had made a fortune in Amway, and the story he and his wife told so motivated Jake that he sat up all night after the rally, preparing a prospect list.

Within a year the Funks' Amway business was profitable enough that Jake left his fuel truck; thirteen years later, he has never been back to that or any other job. He and Helen are Double Diamonds today, and are considered key leaders in the Amway world of Canada. They enjoy the life-style the Delisles described at that Winnipeg rally long ago—the life-style provided by "a six-figure income and no boss."

That really *is* breaking out!

7 Crazy Rallies

NO ASPECT of the Amway world attracts more attention than its large public meetings. "Rallies" they are usually called, or perhaps they are known by other, more colorful labels: "Free Enterprise Day," "Dream Night," "Family Reunion," "Moving-Up Seminar," "Leadership Weekend," and a variety of others.

By whatever name, literally hundreds of these large public gatherings are held in cities across North America on a year-round basis. Crowd size varies from a few hundred people in a hotel ballroom to upwards of 15,000 in a big-city coliseum. The speakers may be bona fide celebrities or merely new Direct Distributors from a nearby town. The event may draw a strictly local audience or attract people from hundreds of miles away; and the event may occupy an entire weekend or only a single two-hour session.

But for all the variety among Amway rallies, virtually all share at least one characteristic: a noisy, happy enthusiasm that some newcomers find exciting, others find bewildering, but no one finds dull. Particularly when the crowd is a large one, the sheer decibel level can be deafening when an Amway rally is in full flow, and media descriptions often emphasize the raucous mood of the crowd more than the significance of the meeting itself. The sight of that many people having that much fun seems to disturb reporters, and their accounts of Amway rallies are often similar in tone to this one, from an article in *Black Enterprise* magazine in late 1981:

A convention atmosphere prevails as the people, wearing buttons and toting cameras, cassettes, and placards, sit in aisles and cram the doorways. The pledge of allegiance is said; preliminary speakers have had their say; and now, sensing that the magic moment is near, the convention yields to a religious fervor as the crowd bursts out with a gospel-type song, one that sets hands clapping and feet to swaying. The featured speakers enter amid flickering flashbulbs and thunderous applause. Attired in tuxedo and full-length mink, they smile and wave as they make their way to the stage.

The tone of that description is familiar to those who read of Amway in the press; a tone of amusement with a touch of condescension. It is, after all, an easier article to write and more interesting to read than a serious explanation of the sales and marketing plan. The giant rally is the most publicly visible aspect of the Amway operation and the most provocative, so it gets lots of attention. There has developed, over a period of years, a public perception that Amway conventions are high-voltage events. The word is out that, when Amway distributors meet, their style is somewhat more energetic than that of, say, the average downtown men's club on Tuesday noon.

The importance of rallies and weekend conventions is deeply rooted in Amway tradition. The corporation itself has always conducted such meetings, going all the way back to the earliest days of the Van Andel-DeVos distributorship. Corporate rallies have become, over the years, more and more sophisticated, and today are high-budget, smoothly operated affairs. They usually include music by the Sanborn Singers, a song-and-dance troupe based in California (of which every member is a Direct Distributor), led by Diamond Directs Fred and Jan Sanborn. Along with the music, there are usually speeches by various corporate officials; speeches by distributors, frequently to tell stories of how they built their businesses; and often a keynote address—sometimes on screen by satellite—by DeVos or Van Andel. Special guest speakers also occasionally appear at such functions; recently these have included such notables as former Treasury Secretary

William E. Simon, economist Milton Friedman, and the popular clergyman Norman Vincent Peale.

Apart from rallies and conventions conducted by Amway Corporation itself, there are hundreds more that are held by individual distributor groups, and it is there that the pattern fragments into the eclectic diversity described earlier. While the corporation watches such meetings carefully and sometimes sends staff representatives to them, Amway itself is not involved in these functions, which tend to be less restrained and more fiercely entrepreneurial in tone. Some Diamond leaders treat the role of impresario quite seriously and conduct meetings of enormous size, with all the glitter and dazzle of a Hollywood opening night.

Big-name entertainers are occasionally part of the drawing card at these events. Bob and Jo Crisp, Atlanta-based Triple Diamonds with a special flair for running glamorous Amway gatherings, have hosted such stars as Johnny Cash and Ray Stevens on their stage. Crisp frequently features sports figures at his meetings, producing such big names as former Notre Dame coach Ara Parseghian, Indiana basketball coach Bobby Knight, and Olympic hockey hero Mike Eruzione —all in 1981.

Art Linkletter and Pat Boone are frequent guests of Amway groups, as are Robert Schuller and Norman Vincent Peale. Political leaders also take their turn at the microphones, recently including former president Gerald R. Ford, senators Jesse Helms of North Carolina and Don Nickles of

Oklahoma, and a plethora of congressmen and local politicians. President Ronald Reagan twice appeared in Charlotte rallies as the guest of Crown Directs Dexter and Birdie Yager, both times prior to becoming president in 1981.

Music, whether imported or locally produced, is an important part of the festivities. A group of Diamonds led by Crown Ambassador Dan Williams conducted a rally in late 1981 that featured Donny and Marie Osmond—and lots of other Osmonds—in a full-length concert at the San Francisco Civic Center. The Osmonds' wholesome, upbeat style fit perfectly the Amway mood that night; they performed encore after encore, then told the crowd, "We've been performing for twenty-five years, and we have honestly never had an audience like this one!" Musical groups such as the Serendipity Singers and the Nashville-based ReGeneration often appear before Amway crowds. Amway distributors who are themselves professional musicians are also popular guests: the country-rock-oriented Sammy Hall Singers; a talented California couple named Don and Peggy Grant, who also work with the Sanborn Singers; and the Delton Alford Singers, a brass-and-vocal group led by Delton and Myrna Alford.

But it is not the speakers and music alone that make Amway evenings memorable. Into the mix of programming is added the crowd, perhaps the most receptive and lively group any speaker or performer will ever stand before; it is the rambunctious enthusiasm of an Amway crowd that makes the occasion memorable. Why are Amway audiences so alive, so responsive, so vocal? Perhaps because they are all volunteers, all there by choice, all agreeing together in the pursuit of their own individual dreams. No one in an Amway crowd has been sent there by a boss; no one is there on assignment, just doing a job. Amway people come together so cheerfully because it is their *own* businesses they come to build; it is their own prospects for the future and achievements of the past that they come to celebrate. It is not the accomplishments of some leader, though they applaud the leader; nor the glories of Amway Corporation, though they embrace the corporation; but the excitement of their own growing businesses, their own freedoms, that brings them together in such a high-spirited atmosphere.

They take something away, too, that makes the meetings worth all the effort. The ultimate purpose of Amway meetings is not show biz, but building distributorships, and Amway's calendar of rallies and weekend conventions apparently pays off on the bottom line. Listening to Amway Diamonds tell their stories, one constantly hears them describe a particular rally or weekend seminar as the single, critical point at which their distributorship was solidified. The example and encouragement of other distributors, perhaps even more than the highly charged speechmaking or the on-stage entertainment, seems to make the total experience a powerful counterpoint to whatever negative pressures the distributor is fighting back home.

"It absolutely makes the difference," states Brian Hays, a Triple Diamond from Chicago who, with his wife Marg, leads one of the largest organizations—and conducts some of the most effective rallies—in the world of Amway. Brian is a former motivation expert from Motorola, with a college degree and years of experience in the area of maximizing performance and work efficiency, so he should know something about the subject.

"It's a new ball game today; it's a new Amway," he declares. "The momentum we have from our growth and from the corporation's growth is showing up in these enormous crowds we are having, and that just makes it grow that much faster. When eight or ten thousand people come together in an auditorium, the impact is terrific. You can do all the talking you want to, but there's something that happens when that new distributor can *see* it. When you can fill up an auditorium that size, it does something that all the talk in the world can't do!

"I love to read history, but it's more fun making history, and I believe that's what we're doing in the world of Amway."

8 Home From the Poconos

A PROMINENT Amway couple who credit a week-end convention with launching their business is Rick and Sue Lynn Setzer. They are Triple Diamonds from Greenville, South Carolina, and members of the Executive Diamond Council; Rick is also a member of the Amway Distributors Association board, a position that establishes him at the top level of field leadership.

The Setzers were schoolteachers before Amway. They lived in a trailer park in a small North Carolina town, got by on the skimpy salaries that are standard for high-school teachers, had begun a family, and had a growing sense that they were making progress toward nowhere. On weeknights they ate dinner, watched television, and went to bed. Weekends were more exciting: they puttered around the trailer on Saturdays and on Saturday nights went window-shopping at the local K-Mart or perhaps took a ride around town. If something good was on television, they stayed home and watched it. On Sundays they went to church, took an afternoon drive through the country-club section of town to see the fancy houses, and dreaded going back to work on Monday.

Rick and Sue Lynn Setzer were in a rut.

A letter from a former fraternity brother, in early 1971, was the catalyst for the Setzers' new life. The old college friend said he had a new part-time business, and would call to tell Rick more about it, which he did. "The time was right," Rick says. "He came over and drew the circles, sitting at our little kitchen table, between the dryer and the stove. It looked pretty good to me, so I asked, 'What do I do next?' Our goal was to make enough money to match Sue Lynn's salary, so she could quit teaching and stay home with David, our son." Sue Lynn was in agreement with the goal, but not with the means of reaching it. The fledgling business grew very little through that spring and by summer was stalled completely.

A weekend seminar in the Pocono Mountains turned things around. "I didn't even want to go," Sue Lynn admits, "but Rick told me I would either go or stay home alone, because he was going, with me or without me. Once I got there, I saw a different way of life. Rick got totally committed to the business that weekend, and when we got home, he didn't slow down for a single day or night until we were Directs. I had another baby a few months later, and while I was in the labor room, Rick

showed the Plan to a policeman he met in the
hospital lobby while we were checking in!"

Sue Lynn was able to leave her job that summer,
and Rick set as a new goal his own retirement a
year later. He worked with an uncommon inten-
sity, once the goal was set. Nothing deflected him.
He had surgery on his back, had a disc removed,
was in the hospital two weeks, and began showing
the Plan again the very day after being discharged.
He encountered a wall of skepticism from his
teaching colleagues; no one thought Amway would
work at all, or if it did, that it would not work for
Setzer. He answered them by making Xerox copies
of his bonus checks and mailing them out as the
monthly amounts grew. That stopped the laughter.
The Setzer business mushroomed: Direct Distributor within six months; Pearl within a year.

He resigned from his job on July 4, 1972, a
double-independence day for the twenty-six-year-
old teacher.

Understandably the Setzers' lives have never
been the same. There are expensive homes instead
of the twelve-by-fifty-two-foot mobile home; there
is a Rolls Royce to replace the old fifty-seven
Chevy pickup truck; there is a constant schedule of
glamorous vacations, in which they usually travel
in their own plane, rather than those Saturday
nights when their entertainment was strolling the
aisles of the local K-Mart.

Other things have changed, in addition to the
material payoffs. "I can see a difference in my

kids since they have a full-time father and mother," Sue Lynn says. "They didn't spend all day with baby-sitters as they would have before, and we believe that has really made a difference." And their friends have changed, they say, with more of their time spent with more positive people. "The most negative place in the world is a teachers' lounge at an average high school," Rick declares. "That negative environment worked on me, and I wanted to get out of it. We like to spend our time with happy, positive people, and for the last ten years we have had the freedom to do that."

So vastly has Amway altered the Setzers' lives, they often reflect on how narrowly they missed not seeing the Plan at all. The pieces fell into place perfectly, to bring that fraternity brother to them at the critical time. Rick's ambition had been to teach at a local community college—had he been given the job, he doubts he would have entertained the business proposal at all. But the college had turned down his job application on Friday; it was two days later that the frat brother called. Rick had not heard from him in four years before that contact.

On the night of their appointment, the meeting very nearly aborted entirely. The friend, driving from out of town, lost his way. He was scheduled to arrive at 7:00 P.M., and by 7:45 had still not found the Setzers' trailer park. He was a new distributor himself and had shown the Plan thirteen consecutive times in the past four months without sponsoring anyone. So, discouraged, he gave up looking for the trailer park and headed home. He passed a pay phone, stopped to call the Setzers to explain, decided to get directions and try again, and this time, an hour late, arrived at their home.

On that slender thread, Rick and Sue Lynn Setzer escaped from that rut, to create for themselves and their family an uncommon freedom.

One hears many such stories, stories in which the fates that bring a person into the Amway orbit seem random and capricious indeed.

Ray and Jackie Newton, who lead a Pearl distributorship in England, took a 1979 vacation to the United States and ran out of gas on a busy highway near Pompano Beach, Florida. An Amway distributor stopped to offer a ride, mentioned his business to them, and found them interested in learning more. They signed on the dotted line, returned to England, and built a thriving business.

Mike Apele, a young Hawaiian with an appetite for travel, was a steward on a commercial airline crew based in Honolulu. His passengers on a flight to Chicago one day included a group of new Direct Distributors on their way to Ada, Michigan. From them he learned about the business, and he and his wife Denise are Diamonds today.

In a quite different climate, on a less glamorous job, another future Diamond was introduced to Amway. Roy Bulmer was a police officer in Ontario who was dispatched to investigate an automobile crash. One of the drivers involved in the accident was an Amway distributor, who, before he was finished, had shown Bulmer more than just his driver's license.

Joe Ferlita, a plant supervisor in Schaumberg, Illinois, was introduced to Amway when his company called in an outside consultant to help raise production levels at his plant. The consultant showed Ferlita how to get higher production from his factory employees and almost casually asked one day if he would be interested in a business of his own. That was fifteen years ago, and as a result of that conversation, Joe and his wife, Mimi, are full-time Diamonds today.

John Turner was a Catholic priest who experienced a long ministry in South America before deciding to leave the priesthood, desiring to marry and have a family. Soon after arriving back in the United States, he was asked by a friend, a former nun, to escort her to a meeting in Fort Lauderdale. It turned out to be an Amway meeting, and though his friend had not tried to sponsor him, he met a young widow named Pat at the convention who did. He at first dismissed the meeting as "a couple of thousand people screaming about something I didn't understand." But as he stayed awhile, and looked more closely, he saw "people who were helping each other, caring for each other." He eventually joined both Amway and his new friend Pat on a full-time basis; they are now happily married Diamonds in Miami.

Many new distributors since 1977 have been introduced to Amway by *The Possible Dream* or *The*

Winner's Circle, two books that have been listed on *The New York Times* best-seller list and have sold millions of copies. Ron and Diane Goldman of Ontario are Emerald Directs with that experience. Goldman was an ambitious salesman who had fallen on hard times and was looking for a new business opportunity.

Browsing through a bookstore one day in Toronto, he picked a copy of *The Possible Dream* off the shelf, bought it, and took it home to read. It sounded like exactly what he was seeking: no capital investment, with unlimited potential. He asked Diane if she knew anyone in the Amway business, and she gave him a name. He made a phone call, asked to be sponsored, and today is a full-time distributor with an aggressive, fast-growing organization.

The book cost Ron Goldman $2.50. No one would argue that he got his money's worth.

9 Such Good Friends

OBVIOUSLY, not everyone who enters Amway does so in such a random and unplanned fashion. If the Amway sales force grew only when a distributor stumbled willy-nilly into a willing prospect, the company would surely not have grown as fast as it has. The majority of new distributors come into the business at the invitation of someone they know and trust. A distributor sponsors a friend, or the friend of a friend, or an acquaintance from the office, or from the PTA, or the local church.

Occasionally the connection is closer than that, when two friends who have shared many things together, over many years, decide to share the attempt to build an Amway business. That combination of an old friendship and a new challenge has, in several prominent cases, resulted in not one but two successful Amway organizations and a friendship even stronger than before.

To onlookers who knew neither couple well, the
Britts and the Renfrows must have seemed poorly
matched to be such good friends. It was the late
1950s when they met in Raleigh, North Carolina.
Peggy Britt and Betty Jo Renfrow worked together
in the secretarial pool at the Carolina Power and
Light Company; their husbands were recently
returned from military service during the Korean
War; Bill Britt was a graduate student at North
Carolina State University and Raleigh's assistant
city manager, while Rex Renfrow worked on the
same campus at an office of the United States
Department of Agriculture. The two couples became close friends. They barbecued steaks on
weekends, attended the same church, went camping and waterskiing together (Rex says, "I had the
tent; he had the boat"), and saw more of each
other than of anyone else. They were what teen-
agers call "best friends."

On the surface, the brotherly bond that developed between Bill and Rex must have seemed an
unlikely one. Britt was then, as now, a take-charge
type, a hard-nosed, no-nonsense leader with emphatic opinions and no reluctance to express them.
Rex, on the other hand, seems at first impression
more subdued, gentler, less aggressive than the
style that Britt favors. Those are the most readily
visible faces of Renfrow and Britt.

A closer look, however, shows each to have another side. Behind the formidable manner of Bill
Britt there is a caring, even a loving person, Renfrow says; Britt may be tough as a ball bearing on

the outside, but he has a heart like a marshmallow. And, conversely, those who know Renfrow will insist that beneath that sweetly smiling surface is a powerful strength of purpose, an iron will that borders on outright stubbornness. Little wonder they got along so well.

Renfrow came naturally to his career in the Department of Agriculture. He grew up on a tobacco farm in North Carolina, went into the navy immediately after high-school graduation, and met Betty Jo while stationed at a navy base in Memphis. She was the youngest of nine children, reared by a widowed mother who "gave us so much love, we never realized how poor we were." After Rex's discharge from the navy, he decided against college in favor of what seemed the greater potential of a career in government service. He began as a clerk-typist (GS-3) in Raleigh and stayed there eleven years, the years when the Renfrows and Britts came to know each other.

In 1966, his career took him away from his home state to New Mexico for a three-year stint, then to South Dakota for two more years, and finally to Washington, D.C. As a government employee (GS-14), he had finally arrived; he was chief of the fiscal branch of the Washington office of the Department of Agriculture. He had moved up a long way; but he realized that, for his level of education, he was at the end of the road. "I had topped out in my career. I knew that I would never be promoted any higher." He was forty years old.

During their years away from North Carolina,

the Renfrows had kept in touch with the Britts, but saw them only on Christmas visits back home. So it was something of a surprise, in October of 1972, when they got a call from Bill, saying that he was in the D. C. area and would stop by to see them that Sunday afternoon. They learned he had resigned from his job as city manager of Goldsboro, North Carolina, and was in a new business. He didn't say what the business was, but asked them to drive down for a visit two weekends later, to find out about it. They went and saw the Amway Plan. Rex didn't fully understand it, he recalls, and Betty Jo hardly even looked. But Bill recommended they give it a try, and "purely out of confidence in him," they did. "I didn't understand the business," Rex says, "but I respected Bill. I knew he wouldn't do anything that wasn't good for me, and I could see he was happy and free. Besides, I was looking for something. I had topped out in my career; inflation was taking me backwards; and I had two children to send through college.

"Bill told me, 'Rex, this is something you've got to accept on faith. You've got to understand that I would not drive two hundred and fifty miles to tell you something that's going to hurt you or cause you to fail. So do what I tell you, and you won't believe how well this thing will work for you within the next year!' So I did it. After I got in, I didn't question that what he was telling me was right. I just did it. We trusted Bill completely."

From their very first meeting together, Britt and Renfrow proved to be as compatible in business as they had been on weekend camping trips. The four of them began spending much of their free time together again—this time with just as much fun, Renfrow says, but with more productive results. The Renfrows' new Amway business grew rapidly from the beginning. They committed several nights each week to it, refusing to slow down even though Rex suffered almost constantly from a protruding disc in his back during much of that first year. The pain in his back made it impossible for Rex to sit normally in an automobile, but he and Betty Jo continued to work their business each night, often showing the Plan to prospects or new distributors who lived many miles away. They traveled those miles with Betty Jo at the wheel and Rex on his knees, sitting backward in the passenger seat, to reduce the pain. He would take a little codeine for the pain just before arriving at the prospects' house, get out and draw the circles, then make the long drive home again.

Britt had promised that such a commitment would pay off within a year, and he was right on schedule. The Renfrows qualified as Ruby Directs one year after they began, became Emeralds less than a year after that, and were Diamonds two and a half years later. They were the first of what would be many Diamonds in the Britt line of sponsorship, and have now helped seven distributorships within their own Amway "family" grow to

Diamond. Their personal ties with the Britts are
stronger than ever, since both couples now have
the time and the money to come and go as they
please. The Britts, who are Triple Diamonds, now
travel in their own private jet, a sleek Citation
loaded with the most advanced aeronautic gear,
with a salaried pilot and copilot—plus a private
helicopter to get them from home to the airport.
That is undoubtedly a notch above the Volkswagen they and the Renfrows drove on weekend
trips in their pre-Amway days.

The Renfrows live on a ten-acre estate in Fair-
fax County, Virginia, complete with horses and
riding stables, tennis court, swimming pool, and
a gazebo-and-patio area, which was a featured
award-winner in *The Washingtonian* magazine in
1981. It is all there: picture-perfect country living
in a posh section of Northern Virginia horse country. And the best thing about it, Rex says, is that
he doesn't have to leave it to go to work every
morning. He left his position at the Department of
Agriculture after he and Betty Jo became Diamonds. The nine-to-five grind was too confining
to him, he explains, and there was little point in
continuing after his Amway income grew to a level
several times his government pay.

"How would you describe the earnings of an
Amway leader such as yourself?" he is asked. He
is understandably reluctant to discuss his income,
but acknowledges that he paid income taxes last
year in six figures. "It's getting to be a lot of

money," he says, smiling, when asked about his income. "Of course it's not even in the ball park with Bill Britt, but it's pretty good for an old country boy without a college education!"

The Renfrows feel that they are just now hitting full stride as Amway leaders, that the spectacular growth they enjoyed in the 1970s will be exceeded in the 1980s. Does their personal involvement with new distributors diminish as they become more successful? "Not at all!" Rex insists. "I love this business. Sure, it's hard work, but most folks I know enjoy hard work, as long as they're being rewarded for it. I don't think I'll ever get to where I don't enjoy bringing new distributors into this business and helping them grow. We talk about duplication in Amway—meaning the way a person sees his own pattern duplicated in the people he sponsors. Well, I would like to think I am duplicating Bill Britt's pattern in my business and my distributors are duplicating me. I'd like to be as good a sponsor to them as the Britts were to us.

"When we sponsor a new distributor, we don't just give them a kit and leave. I make a commitment to everyone I sponsor: 'If you will give this thing your best, I'll give you my best. I'll work harder than you will. I'll stay up later than you will. I'll drive more miles; I'll talk more hours; I'll invest more time; I'll do more in every area than you will, to help *you* to be successful in this business. If it takes you ten years to go Direct, as long as you're hanging in there, I'll hang in there with you. I won't quit until you do. And if you don't believe it, try me!' ''

It is a powerful challenge. Coming from Rex Renfrow, it has a conviction about it that is almost irresistible. His track record shows he means every word of it.

10 Opportunity Knocks

WITH ALL THIS emphasis on finding and persuading prospective distributors, it is apparent that not many fish actually jump into the net. But some do.

Bob and Terry Andrews did. They are in Amway because they sought out someone to sponsor them. The Andrewses, two of the whiz kids of the business, reached the level of Crown Direct while barely in their thirties. They became distributors when they were still single; Bob was twenty-three years old; Terry was nineteen.

The couple were students at the University of South Florida, eager to get married, but with the common undergrad problem of no money. Terry's father was a practical-minded man who responded to Bob's romantic yearnings by having him fold a sheet of paper in half, list all his income on one side and his expenses on the other. "When those two columns match," he said, "you'll be ready to get married." So Bob and Terry began looking for something they could do—preferably together—to earn a living, get married, and stay in school. They searched the classified ads for weeks, with no results.

It was during this time that Bob's cousin came to visit and advised the love-struck twosome: "You should take a look at that thing called Amway. I have some friends who are in it, and from what they tell me about it, you'd be good at that sort of thing." The cousin was not a distributor and never became one, but Bob and Terry acted on his suggestion and went out in search of someone to sponsor them into Amway.

One of Bob's old schoolteachers—sixth- and seventh-grade math—had become an Amway distributor, they had heard, so they called him. His name was Dusty Owens. They didn't realize it at the time, but Dusty and Betty, his wife, had built a Double Diamond business right there in Tampa. "We'd like you to help us to make some extra money so we can get married," Bob explained. Dusty was busy, but agreed to talk with them, and two weeks later invited them to his house to hear the plan. Bob showed up that day in jeans and a faded Army fatigue jacket; he wore long hair and beads in the accepted, campus style. He was not an especially promising prospect, this hippy-looking college boy with his teenage girl friend, but Dusty and Betty dutifully sat down at a card table and drew the circles out on a napkin.

After they saw the Plan, Bob and Terry asked if they could go outside and talk it over before making a decision. They walked out to the driveway, leaned against the sixty-eight Chevelle Bob drove, and decided they had nothing to lose. "It looks pretty good to me," Bob said. "We'll never know if we don't try it," Terry answered. So they tromped summarily back inside and signed up. Bob went home that night and borrowed the money from his mother to buy the kit, confidently telling her that he had found a way to earn enough extra money to make the monthly $73.50 payment on his Chevelle.

It was an unpromising beginning. Terry still lived in the dorm at the university; Bob lived at home with his parents. They used the trunk of the Chevelle as their office-cum-warehouse and hung their first sales plaque there, right above the adding machine and the products. But they sold enough products personally, that first month, to earn $150, and in an orgy of thrift sank it all into double car payments. Their retail business grew every month; they began sponsoring a few people; and a few months later were married on faith that their business would pay the bills.

It always has. Bob had done practice teaching in college as a music teacher, but "bailed out as soon as I got my Amway income where it needed to be. I loved teaching music, but the money just wasn't there. I spent more time hassling with administrators over the length of my hair than I did teaching students. So I quit all that other stuff; I burned my bridges. I want to make this business my life.''

Contrasting sharply with the Andrewses' experience of finding Amway is the story of Crown Ambassadors Chuck and Jean Strehli, who literally had Amway come knocking on their door and turned it down.

The Strehlis are an attractive Texas couple who are among Amway's best-known and most admired leaders. They live in Austin, home of the University of Texas, and like the Andrewses, were students when they first heard about the business. Chuck was in his second year of law school; Jean was a dietician in the traditional role of working hubby through school. They lived in a converted World War II barracks building that the university had pressed into service as housing for married students. Chuck was studying one afternoon in the little apartment, heard a knock on the door, and shuffled over to answer it. He was wearing bermuda shorts and a pair of flip-flop shower shoes.

He remembers it well: ''I opened the door, and there stood this total stranger with a big smile and a big black bag.'' He reached into the bag, pulled out an aerosol can, and sprayed it into the air. Taking one quick glance downward at Strehli's undershod feet, he dived again into his bag, extracted a second spray can, and carefully sprayed the offending feet from ankle to toe. Then he made a little speech about the wonderful world of

Amway and its terrific income opportunities.

Strehli was broke, but he wasn't *that* broke. *If this is Opportunity knocking,* he figured, *I'll pretend I'm not home.*

A month later he got another chance. Flipping through the newspaper ads one day, he saw a part-time-job offer. Or at least that's what he thought he saw. It was before the days of Amway Corporation's tight control over the content of such ads; and when Chuck answered the ad and scheduled an interview, he expected to be hired as a part-time employee for some sort of marketing firm. He stuffed a resumé in his pocket and left for the appointment, intending to ask for a starting salary of $125 per month.

What he got was better. The Amway distributor he met that day offered him not a job, but a challenge: "If I could show you a way to make a thousand dollars a month in your spare time, would you be willing to give up your spare time for it?" It was a great question, and Chuck was hooked by it. He decided that afternoon to try the business and see if it worked. Jean, when she heard about it, was adamantly opposed. "I am a classic example of a negative wife who had to be overcome," she admits. "I reacted to Chuck with one sentence. I told him, 'Chuck, I will never sell *anything* to *anybody* at *anytime!*' "

But she relented, as those first few months passed, and if she was indeed a "classic example of a negative wife" at the outset, she would be regarded by many as the near-perfect Amway partner today. The Strehlis set as a first goal the achievement of the three things most important to Jean: to live in a better apartment (''anything with a front door and a back door''), to quit her job (''I hated it''), and to start a family. If she would work with him, Chuck promised her, they would go for those goals first. She agreed, and within eleven months had reached all three.

Since then, the rewards have become more glamorous. They have lived out many of their dreams, including a seven-month working vacation in Munich, Germany, for the entire family. Chuck finished law school, but never practiced law; by graduation time, it just didn't make economic sense to do so. Despite her hard work to get him through law school, Jean approves heartily of having a nonlawyer husband. ''It's terrific to work together, husband and wife. When the phone rings and someone asks 'Is Chuck there?' I say to them, 'No, but this is Jean; may I help you?' And I *do* help them. Can you imagine that exchange occurring if Chuck were a lawyer?!''

So there are those college students who found Amway, like the Andrewses, and those who were found by it, like the Strehlis. But there is one final example: a case where not once, not twice, but three times the Amway opportunity came knocking, and every time Bill Hicks answered the door.

This time the campus was the University of Alabama, at Tuscaloosa. Home of Paul ''Bear''

Bryant and the Crimson Tide football team. Bill
Hicks did not play football at Alabama; he played
soldier. He was an ROTC undergraduate, in 1964,
when a fellow student offered him an opportunity
to sell shoe spray to his ROTC friends as an Amway distributor. He did so for the next two years,
but dropped his distributorship without a second
thought when he graduated and left the campus.

Five years later, Hicks was married and working, but still wearing a uniform and thus still in
need of that high-gloss shine on his boots. (This
time it was the Alabama National Guard.) So
when a friend asked him if he wanted to make
some extra money in Amway, Hicks replied,
"Sure, I've done that before. Send me a few cases
of that shoe spray." So once again he became a
distributor, and once again he totally missed the
full potential of his business. He attended no
meetings, held no meetings, attempted to sponsor
no one at all. But he sold a lot of shoe spray, and
all his National Guard buddies had great-looking
boots.

In 1973 Bill and Becky were living in the Atlanta
area, transferred there in his job with an insulation
company. A friend from Birmingham offered to
show him the Amway Plan one day, and Hicks
flatly refused. "I told him I already knew all about
it, and I wasn't interested. Period. I figured I had
already done that, and didn't care about selling
any more shoe spray. But three months later, that
friend of mine was doing so well and making so
much money that I knew there must be more to it

than I knew about, so I literally begged him to show me what it was he was doing.''

The third time was the charm. To those skeptics who worry about Amway "saturation" and compute the number of people who have already tried Amway and presumably are no longer candidates for the business, Bill and Becky Hicks must surely confuse the statistics. They had been distributors, after a fashion, not once, but twice. But the third time they captured the dream of Amway and were ready in their own personal development to make the dream come true. Today they are Diamonds, still very young, with a very bright future ahead of them in Amway. And perhaps a part of their success is due to their special understanding of those distributors who falter at first, who are in and out and in again, before their dream finally takes shape.

Opportunity didn't just knock for Bill Hicks; it hung around the front porch, until finally Bill invited it in to stay.

11 Wonder Woman

WOMEN IN AMERICA have never had it so good.

After many generations of rigid female social roles, women finally have options they have never had before. No longer is there the single inflexible expectation that their mothers and grandmothers faced, that of home and hearth and helping hubby. In its place, the modern woman chooses from a wide range of options: career woman, creative homemaker, partner in her husband's business or operator of a business of her own. Like their male counterparts, women now can choose the roles which best suit their own inclinations.

The roles chosen by women in Amway are equally diverse. The prototype of the Amway distributorship is that of a married couple, with the husband taking the lead and the wife playing a supportive role; but there are so many exceptions to that model that the model itself can be misleading. Amway Corporation works tirelessly to insure that both spouses in a distributorship are given equal treatment and equal billing. There are no separate rewards for the husbands, no separate recognition for one spouse over the other. The distributorship belongs equally to both partners, the corporation insists; how you divide the work is up to you, but how we divide the rewards is up to us, and we intend to divide them evenly.

That policy, along with the very nature of the business itself, gives the women of Amway a highly visible presence that most find refreshingly different from the "other job" their husbands have. Not only is the critically important role of the wife in a husband-wife partnership recognized, it is underscored and highlighted. "I think it's terrific," one Amway wife declares, "that Amway understands that the women in this business contribute just as much as their husbands do and that the company gives us credit for it. A successful Amway business is usually as much the woman's achievement as it is her husband's."

Sometimes even more so.

The Yamada distributorship, for example. Frank and Karen Yamada have established a business in which they share the work and rewards, but both acknowledge that it is she who provided the original impetus for its growth and who has always accepted the most publicly visible leadership role. Such a division of roles in the Yamada distributorship is no accident; it is a style of operating their business that has been carefully and shrewdly designed to fit into their life as a family, and it works exceptionally well.

But the Yamadas are an exceptional couple. Frank is a dentist whose father emigrated to America from the Japanese farming state of Wakayama, in 1917. The elder Mr. Yamada eventually settled in California, where Frank was born. Karen is a third-generation Japanese-American who grew up in Idaho with all Caucasian schoolmates, speaks no Japanese, and says, "I never really knew what it meant to be Japanese until I met Frank." That was in 1960, the same year he entered dental school at Washington University in St. Louis.

Four years later, the young couple settled in Orange County, California, to open Frank's dental practice. For the next ten years, Karen stayed busy with the charitable and civic activities one expects from the energetic wife of a successful dentist. In the mid-1970s Frank suffered a coronary attack and recovered from it; and perhaps coincidentally, more of Karen's activity turned toward business projects rather than community ones. Her partner in these businesses was Eunice Fujimoto, a close friend from dental school. For the most part, their ventures turned out to be wonderful failures; Karen and Eunice had lots of fun playing at being businesswomen, while Frank and Gil (Eunice's husband) footed the bills. The two wives tried a bit of everything: real estate, auto-mechanic's school, a tailoring business. In all of it they cheerfully, though unintentionally, maintained their non-profit status.

So it was that an invitation to see a business opportunity, from yet a *third* dentist's wife, was not unusual. Karen went and was not particularly impressed. "I thought it sounded like a very nice business, but I really didn't think it was for me," she recalls. But the next day she dropped by the Fujimotos' and explained it to them, and to Karen's surprise, they responded with immediate enthusiasm. "You ought to do this, Karen," Eunice said, "and we'll do it with you." So they did, with their husbands gallantly supporting them. "She was always busy doing something," Frank explains, "and this seemed no different. I thought it was just another little woman's thing for Karen, that's all."

Some "little woman's thing" it turned out to be! Karen plunged into the new business with dazzling success. She kept a full calendar. While Frank carried the load for her in the financial management and organizational chores of the business, he gave Karen full support while she showed the Plan and conducted the meetings and training sessions. "I made a commitment to the business," Frank says, "but Karen does the circles; she does the speaking. I've done three big home meetings, and they were disasters."

But Frank was more than just an observer, Karen points out, and together they developed a pattern that yielded unusually positive results.

They went Direct in ninety days, were Pearls in their seventh month, Emeralds in their thirteenth month, and two years after coming into Amway, in June of 1980, qualified as Diamond Directs.

The Yamada distributorship is remarkable not only for its dramatic growth, but also for its heavily Asian-American makeup, especially at the higher pin levels. The Yamadas estimate that one-third of their group are of Asian ancestry, a percentage that at an earlier time was even higher. It is the largest Amway group of Asian-Americans on the mainland United States, and all the Pearl and Emerald distributorships within the group, except one, are Asian. "I have great pride in that," Karen admits. "I am proud that we can do the business so well. I like being in the Asian community here in California. I want my kids to have a greater sense of being Asian, and I like the idea of cultivating a large Asian business." Frank agrees: "When you have a racial or ethnic heritage, such as we do, you should maintain it. You should understand it and be proud of it. That is certainly the way we feel in our family and in our Amway group."

Another thing Frank Yamada is proud of is the unusual ability of his wife and her leadership in their business. "She is a fighter," he says of Karen. "She took it as a challenge to show that a woman could build a great Amway business. We don't consider it *her* business; we consider it *our* business; but I'm proud of the fact that she has taken the lead in building it. As time goes on, I have become more and more involved, but in the beginning I didn't even go to the rallies. She really deserves the credit for what has been accomplished, and I'm proud of her for it."

What about the other men in the Yamadas' Amway "family"? Do they ever resent being led by a woman? "Not at all. In fact, the men in our business are pretty protective of the women," Frank says. "That hasn't been a problem at all," Karen chimes in. "That's one of the great things about this business. People respect achievement, regardless of who does it."

Perhaps that hackneyed phrase, "liberated woman," has been so overused and abused that it is hardly worth using at all anymore. But if the phrase has any meaning, then surely, in its very best sense, it describes Karen Yamada. She has remarkable energy and talent. She has an intelligent and self-assured husband who enjoys successes enough of his own not to be threatened by hers. Together they have an Amway business that pays off purely on the basis of achievement.

It would be difficult to improve on that combination.

12 Pacific

ON ANY GIVEN day, at noon, when workers at the Ada office are sitting down to lunch, Amway people in Germany and France are already beginning their 7:00 P.M. meetings; Alaskan and Hawaiian Directs are just yawning their way into the new day; and distributors in Kuala Lumpur, Malaysia, their work already done for another day, are fast asleep at midnight. At any given moment, twenty-four hours every day, somewhere on the globe, Amway products are being sold, and Amway circles are being drawn.

The Amway experience is a genuinely cross-cultural one. The business thrives in the United Kingdom, most of the countries of Western Europe, Australia, Bermuda, Japan, Hong Kong, and Malaysia; and Taiwan is opening as an Amway market in early 1982. To date, the international track record is perfect: the Amway business

has successfully taken root in every country into
which it has ventured. International sales volume,
in fact, has grown faster than domestic activity in
the past two years.

International expansion began with Australia in
1970, moved to England and Europe in 1972, and
entered Asia with the opening of a Hong Kong office in 1974. The attempt to create an Amway
presence in Hong Kong figured to be a difficult
one. The population is multicultural, and both
Chinese and English are employed as official
languages. Over 5 million people are crowded on
the 200 islands that make up Hong Kong. Direct-
sales companies have traditionally had a tough
time there; Avon, for example, *withdrew* from
Hong Kong in 1981. The average home or apartment is tiny, by United States standards, making
product storage difficult for most distributors.
Personal ownership of automobiles is also relatively unusual, with public transportation the most
common way of moving about.

So it was not surprising to Laurie Mulham, the
Amway executive vice-president who supervised
expansion in the Pacific, that the company started
slowly in Hong Kong. For the first few years, no
distributor reached the level of Direct, and the corporation lost money steadily. Van Andel, DeVos
and Mulham were patient—they *had* to be, in this
case—and they have been rewarded in the early
1980s by a virtual explosion of growth in the Hong
Kong market; the turnaround there is one of Amway's most dramatic success stories. Eva Cheng,

the first female general manager in Amway Corporation, runs the Hong Kong operation, and is given much of the credit, by local distributors and Ada officials alike, for the strong upsurge.

An estimated one-quarter of approximately ten thousand Hong Kong distributors speak English, and virtually all company materials are printed in both Chinese and English. Typical of the field leaders who are emerging in Hong Kong is Arthur Li, who, with his wife, Juni, are Diamonds after only three years in the business. Juni was born in Shanghai, on the Communial Chinese mainland and fled to Hong Kong in 1958, at the age of thirteen. She is a librarian; Arthur is an insurance executive and an import-export broker who was sponsored by a relative who had moved to California some years earlier.

Hong Kong's first Double Diamonds were Daniel and Wendy Ng; like Arthur Li, they were sponsored in 1978 by a friend from the United States. Daniel, whose job with American Express Company gave him numerous business contacts in Hong Kong, made an all-out assault on Amway success from the beginning. He made a pact with himself not to go home from work each evening until he had shared the Amway Plan with at least one person. No exceptions. The persistent Mr. Ng recalls that he broke that pledge only a few times in two years, and as a result, he and Wendy became Direct Distributors within ten months and full-time Double Diamonds within three years.

• • •

The course of the business in Malaysia followed a quite different path. If Hong Kong was the proverbial tortoise in its early days, Malaysia was the hare. Business in that country began informally as a branch of the Hong Kong office, largely on the initiative of a Singapore businessman who saw the potential in Malaysia before Amway Corporation did. When the Malaysian operation was officially opened in 1978, distributors there were already poised for a period of spectacular growth that still continues.

The corporation's general manager in Kuala Lumpur, L. K. Choong, has directed Amway's development there from the beginning. "I think we can maintain our growth rate," he says. "There is good balance in our distributor force, and we have the kind of leaders who give us great credibility." Among the leaders to whom he refers is Tan Siew Lan, a Chinese schoolteacher who could speak no English when she entered Amway and lived 150 miles from the nearest source of products. She built a Diamondship, nonetheless—the first single woman in the world of Amway to do so.

Malaysia's first Double Diamonds were Gerry and Angela DeSilva. He is a dental surgeon who, like many young Malaysians, went to England to study, graduating from the University of London Royal College of Surgeons. It was in London that he met Angela, a young Chinese woman from Singapore, who was a graduate student in geography. They married and returned to Kuala Lum-

pur, he to practice dentistry, she to teach, which
they did for the next sixteen years. They heard
about Amway from a friend who was their insurance agent. Angela went to his office to report an
auto accident, was shown the Plan, and signed up
on the spot. "We had not seen a single product
and didn't really understand the Plan," Angela
remembers, "we signed up on blind faith in our
friend." When the trusting Mrs. DeSilva informed
her husband that "we have a new business," he set
out to find out whatever he could about Amway.

Gerry DeSilva is a thorough man. First, he
wrote a letter of inquiry to the editor of the _Finan-
cial Times_ in London, only half-expecting a reply.
Two weeks later the editor's answer came, con-
firming that Amway was an "honest company"
and was doing well in England. Still not wholly
satisfied, DeSilva went to the United States Em-
bassy and asked a staff member in the Trade
Division what he knew about an American company named Amway. "Never heard of it!" the em-
bassy official responded, but proceeded to look
for a report in a State Department reference book;
he returned to tell DeSilva that there was indeed an
Amway in the United States, and that it had "a
five-star rating, the best rating they give."

Finally convinced, the DeSilvas plunged head-
long into the challenge of building a profitable
distributorship. Dr. DeSilva is a well-known man
in Kuala Lumpur; he is a past president of the
Malaysian Dental Association and was a member
of the first dental team ever to visit Communist

China, in 1973. His office is in the Malaysian capital's most fashionable district, and his clientele included twelve ambassadors at the time he entered the business. "I had to clear myself of my own status hangups," he admits. "We realized that if we wanted to do this business, we must be willing to open our lives to people of every station —no matter their status in life." And they have done that, sponsoring new distributors from every part of the socioeconomic spectrum. Their upperclass connections are still firmly in place, but even as they lunch at the elegant old Club of Selangor, home of Kuala Lumpur's elite society, they speak fondly of new friends—a welder, a foundry worker, a waiter—all members of their Amway "family." They say the business has opened them up to a broader and better way of looking at other people, and it is evident that they enjoy their changed perspective.

Leaders with the depth and experience of the DeSilvas, Ngs, and Lis have not had time to emerge in the relatively new Amway operation in Japan. "The Japanese potential is incredible," a corporation official in Ada asserts. "The Japanese are generally very astute business people, and we expect a strong distributor force to develop there."

Amway entered Japan in 1979 and at present operates with an abbreviated product line (twenty-seven products) and a distributor force in which the level of Diamond is the highest pin level so far reached. That pin belongs to Yoko Wada, an impressive young distributor who heard about Amway from "a friend of a friend" whom she met in a supermarket two years ago. She lives in Yokohama, and is the wife of a professor of marine biology and mother of two preschool children. "People in Japan have seen the good life and don't want to give it up," she says. "The cost of living is going up faster than the income in Japan. Amway gives a way to respond to that problem."

One of Yoko's own motivations for building a business is her desire to send her children to a private Catholic school, where tuition rates are extremely high. She was educated in a convent in Belfast, Ireland, traveling there as a sixteen-year-old, to learn English. From Belfast, she went to France to study cooking and returned home to teach in a cooking school in her native Tokyo. "Japanese women are generally not as independent as American or European women," she reflects. "That is a good thing this business brings. It helps make women more independent, and that is much needed in this country."

Though Yoko Wada speaks fluent English, most of her fellow distributors do not, and the translation of more Amway sales and promotional materials into the Japanese language is a major priority of the corporation there. As that process continues, as the maze of governmental red tape is cut in the new market, and as more and more leaders such as Yoko Wada emerge, no one doubts that the Land of the Rising Sun will be an Amway operation of enormous size. And even today, the translation problem is not an insurmountable one.

Andre Blanchard, the French Canadian leader who pioneered the growth of Amway in Quebec, knows all about language barriers, and how they can be broken. "Fortunately," he is fond of saying, "money is bilingual!"

13 Metamorphosis

METAMORPHOSIS. Growth and maturity. The caterpillar becomes the butterfly. The rookie becomes a seasoned veteran. A new, better form emerges from an earlier one. The brilliant newcomer develops into a leader of substance.

That is the pattern of Amway's coming of age in the late 1970s and early 1980s. The company has not only grown, but has matured. No longer the flash and dazzle of the *nouveau riche*, but a more solid respectability and a more sure-footed leadership within the industrial and corporate community. Amway, as it grows into the eighties, has not merely become bigger; it has become better. It is fulfilling the promise of its earlier days.

That metamorphosis, while true of Amway as a whole, also describes many of its distributors individually. Don Held is one of them. He is a Diamond Direct from Ohio, a typical example of the high-energy, ambitious young businessmen who were attracted to Amway many years ago and have developed and matured along with the company. Held was a successful distributor almost from the beginning, but in the early days of his Amway career, thirteen years ago, he succeeded by sheer force of a contagiously cheerful personality and an enormous appetite for hard work. His Amway friends called him Mr. Excitement, and he bounded from place to place, exuding a level of enthusiasm that was rare even in Amway, where enthusiasm is the norm. He had been an IBM employee, but had quickly developed an Amway business of sufficient size to support him full-time. He became an Emerald, made a good living, and directed an organization that duplicated his own cheerful and rambunctious style. He was Mr. Excitement.

But within the past few years, the exuberant bursts of energy so typical of Don Held have developed a smooth and reliable rhythm, and his Amway business has matured correspondingly. There is now efficiency to go along with the effervescence; the "ain't it great" enthusiasm has acquired depth and resonance. Like Amway Corporation itself, Don Held's business has become not just older, but bigger and better as the years have passed. Today it represents the many Amway distributorships around the country that have become solid, well-organized businesses without losing the freshness and zeal that give momentum to the whole thing.

Held lives in a fashionable suburb outside Columbus, Ohio, just a short five-iron shot from the famous Muirfield Village Country Club. He enjoys the typical trappings of affluence: a private twin-engine plane; expensive cars; a game room for the kids, complete with electronic video games; salaried staff members for the nuts-and-bolts operation of his business; and a fat portfolio of investments. Even his spending patterns show a gradual change from earlier years, with admittedly less of his money going to consumer items and more of it to long-range investments and philanthropic giving. "Sure, we enjoy the furs and the diamonds and the cars," Held says. "We have those things, and it's still fun to have them, but that doesn't really turn us on, anymore, as much as the more substantial things do. We enjoy supporting the causes we believe in, and we're making the kind of money that allows us to do that. I think that's what really turns us on most."

The "we" to which Held refers includes his wife, Georgia, a trim and stylish beauty who is in every sense a full partner in the Held distributorship. Those who know the Helds well say that Georgia deserves much of the credit for the couple's success, that she is a shrewd administrator who provides a perfect balance to her husband's more flamboyant style. She is an organizer who knows how to get a job done; he is an extraordinary motivator and inspirational leader. Together they are quite a team.

The Helds married six years ago, after a courtship that began when he sponsored her into Amway. He was already an Emerald at the time, raising four sons alone after an earlier marriage had gone awry. Georgia worked in the office of Don's attorney, with an eight-year career as a legal secretary and a special feminine toughness that she attributes to her childhood as an Air Force officer's kid. She had two children from a previous marriage and fell in love not only with Held, but with his business as well. "What I loved about this business," she reflects, "was the emotion and the real, honest love I felt. It was such a contrast to anything I had known before. I loved the people and the way they were willing to show how they cared for each other."

Georgia found in her Amway partnership with Don Held a feminine role that was ideal for her. "This business gave me an opportunity to develop my creative energies and still be domestic as much as I wish. Don takes the lead, and I like that. I was pretty independent. I had lived alone and had raised my babies all by myself. I had to learn to trust Don and let him take the lead, and that's the way it has been with us. Do I miss my career? Not at all. In this business I make a big contribution, and I get plenty of recognition for that. So many women think they have to go out and seek something to be important in. Well, this business offers that. You can make a major contribution, and you know that what you're doing is important to thousands of people."

Apparently so, at least in the Helds' case. Their

Amway organization of over ten thousand active distributors include several thousand Canadians, and meetings conducted by the Columbus couple attract thousands of people from all over North America. The Helds' deep commitment to a conservative political philosophy is reflected among their distributors. "Our American Christian heritage is really the theme of it all," Held says. "Our cause and purpose go far beyond making money. We believe that people work hardest when they're motivated by a cause they really believe in, and not just by money. We emphasize our American heritage in our group. We believe it's important. We have been making a great income for several years, but we were going in circles politically. We feel we have found a structure for our political beliefs, and we've spent a lot of time and money to spread these ideas to others. It's not a partisan thing at all. We're not primarily concerned with a particular political party or a particular candidate. We introduce people to the concept of commitment to the goals and values that undergird this country. We think that's important, and we are personally committed to that cause."

Does that distract from their Amway business?

"Not at all!" smiles the irrepressible Don Held. "In fact, the very opposite has happened. Our business has just exploded; it's grown so fast. We have found that people will only work so much for personal gain and profit. To operate at their very best, people must have a cause to work for. That's what makes Amway so great: it's not just personal gain, but a cause that lies behind what we do. Our people are better informed than ever before. They are getting real substance in what they hear from us now, not just a lot of crispy-crackly motivational speeches.''

Whether it is the influence of a good cause, the presence of a skillful woman, or simply the advantage of greater experience, one thing is sure: the Held organization is a more effective, more mature Amway force than ever before. ''No doubt about it,'' Don agrees. ''We have more teaching; we have a better pattern. We know what we're doing. A few years back, people used to 'believe' so much they would practically vibrate, but they didn't know what to do next. Now we know what to do. We're still excited, but now we know what to do about it.''

14 When Bad Things Happen . . .

A POPULAR song lyric, many years ago, made a suggestion:

> Ac-cent-tchu-ate the positive,
> E-lim-my-nate the negative,
> Don't mess with Mister Inbetween.

Stories about Amway people follow that advice. Amway talk sometimes seems to be all "happy talk"; it sounds as if Amway Diamonds skip cheerfully from one successful event in their lives to another, with nary a negative moment to break or spoil the fun. "Don't *bad* things ever happen to these people?" an exasperated editor once asked after a long evening of hearing Amway stories.

Bad things happen to all good people, and Amway people are of course no exception. Even in Amway, accidents occur, children get sick, businesses and marriages fail, people die; the entire range of bad things still happen to good people, Amway or not. But often, when things do go wrong, the results are different in a family determined to "accentuate the positive."

If someone should create a Hall of Fame of Amway's bright young couples, John and Jennie Belle Crowe would surely be near the top of the list. They are a young and attractive couple who made a major commitment of time to their Amway business while still in their twenties. They have an intense desire to be free, and Amway became the means of getting there. "I figured if I was willing to give forty years of my life to some corporation, I ought at least to be willing to give five years to my own dream," John said. "I didn't want to let some pay scale tell me whether or not my wife had to work, how many children I could have, where I could live, and how much of life I could afford."

John Crowe didn't get into Amway to quit. He got in to become a free man, and that is exactly what happened. It took a while for the Crowes to find the handle. They shared the Plan with almost fifty people in the Northern Virginia area where they lived and sponsored only one. The first weekend conference they attended was in Wilmington, North Carolina, and they went, even though they had no spare cash to make the trip. They remember borrowing coins from a brother's piggy bank to pay bridge tolls en route. They took peanut butter and jelly with them and made sandwiches to eat in their room when the banquet meals were served. It was July; they drove an old Capri with no air conditioning, had a flat tire to compound the frustration—and when they arrived home that weekend, despite the problems, they were exuberant about their new Amway business.

With that kind of commitment, things of course got better. As the Crowe distributorship grew and their financial situation improved, they began to have the money for things they couldn't afford before. Little things meant a lot. Jennie Belle recalls: "We were sitting at breakfast in a restaurant one morning, out in California, in Napa Valley, and John ordered two milks with breakfast. I sat there thinking about how wonderful our lives were and how God had blessed us, and I suddenly realized that in all the years we dated and in three years of marriage, he had never ordered *two milks!* We just never could afford it before—to be in a place like that and order whatever we wanted. I just sat there and cried, and when I told John what I was crying about, he cried, too. It sounds so silly now, such a simple thing like two milks, but that morning, somehow, it reminded me how far we had come."

At the age of twenty-seven, John resigned from his engineering job to go full-time, and at thirty moved with his young family to a twenty-five-acre country estate in Loudoun County, Virginia, near Washington D.C.

It was on a Monday night, after midnight, on June 16, 1981, that John Crowe almost died. Jennie Belle and the children were visiting relatives in North Carolina that night, and John had been working late. As he entered a side door of the brick farmhouse, Crowe was surprised by two men who had been hiding in shrubbery near the door. The assailants were armed; they forced Crowe inside and began to ransack the house. Crowe resisted the two burglars, and in the brief struggle, one of them shot him, at close range, in the head.

When the police arrived, Crowe showed no vital signs. He was airlifted by Maryland State Police helicopter to the shock-trauma unit of Suburban Hospital in Bethesda, Maryland. He went into emergency surgery for his head wound and after three hours was rolled out of the operating room into the intensive-care unit, listed in critical condition.

Almost immediately after the shooting, Crowe's Amway "family" swung into action. A call went out to his associates; the word spread with incredible speed along the Amway network. His upline mentor, Bill Britt, sent his private plane to pick up Jennie Belle and other family members and rush them to John's bedside. The Crowes' fellow Diamonds converged on Bethesda; by the next morning many top Amway leaders in the area were there, and so many phone calls, telegrams, flowers, and offers of help poured into the hospital that word was sent out to "please stop!"

To Jennie Belle, the Diamonds in that hospital waiting room offered help of a more substantial form than just sympathy and good wishes. They created a cash fund to pay the bills. No big deal, no extended appeals for contributions; they quietly passed the hat and put together enough money, on the spot, to cover any needs that Jennie Belle might encounter in what all knew would be a long ordeal. They also gave their time. Someone produced a calendar, and the Diamonds, all highly skilled Amway professionals, disrupted their own plans, and committed large chunks of time to do the things John would normally have done, to keep his business growing and to keep the burden of managing it off Jennie Belle's shoulders while John recovered.

John did recover. He fought back from the injury and all the related medical problems that it produced, to return home to his family and his business again. He fought his injuries with the same tenacity and courage with which he did everything in life, and while he did so, he and his wife received the kind of support money can't buy. Ironically, in one of those moments of unexplained premonition, John had once talked of just such a situation, while speaking to a large Amway crowd the previous November. He spoke of the love and support that Amway friends give to one another in times of trouble and particularly of his love for his fellow Diamonds in his group. "You know what's the greatest thing about this business

to me?'' he said that night. ''The greatest thing is
to know that if something should happen to me,
Jennie will never be alone!''

And she wasn't.

Few things are more dramatic than for a vigorous young man to be shot down in his own
home, but there are many other cases of Amway
people who wade through waters just as deep, in
an endless variety of circumstances. There is another young couple in Amway, on the other side of
the country, who have also faced what seemed, at
the time, almost overwhelming adversity. And for
them, as for the Crowes, the Amway connection
made an important difference.

Jim and Nancy Dornan live in Orange County,
California, transplants from the Midwest. Jim was
an engineer, a Purdue graduate who says he realized after being out of college only one year that he
was trained to do a job he didn't enjoy, and one
that would not get him where he wanted to go in
life. When someone told them about Amway, they
were actively looking for an alternative to their
jobs (Nancy was a speech therapist) and started a
distributorship even though it seemed ''really an
uncomfortable thing'' for them to try. ''Our beginning was pathetic,'' Nancy insists, though the
record shows that they became Directs after only
ten months.

''We made it because we had a keen desire to
live differently,'' Jim says. ''We looked at the
people who were doing well in Amway, and we

liked what we saw. There was a positive atmosphere, no bellyaching, and a terrific life-style." When they made Direct, he quit his job at Douglas Aircraft, in Long Beach. "As soon as I had enough money to buy my freedom, I bought it," he explains. "It came pretty cheap back then."

In 1974, the carefree life of the engaging young California couple was changed and challenged by an unforeseeable event. Nancy gave birth to a son; they named him Eric. But Eric did not come home right away. He was born with a severe birth defect, an open spine condition that kept him in the hospital for the first nine months of his life. For those nine months—and many more afterward—Eric's physical condition was the dominant reality in the Dornans' life. He was taken to an operating room for surgery eighteen times—fifteen of them involving open-brain procedures. He spent most of the time between operations encased in a full-length cast, from chest to toes.

Those nine months were an "almost unbelievable" experience for the Dornans. They practically lived at the hospital. Twice the parents were told he would not live. "There never seemed to be any relief from the stress," Nancy says.

Through the whole experience, the thing that made the ordeal manageable, according to the Dornans, was their Amway business. "Being in the business made all the difference. We didn't have to worry about paying the bills or keeping things going. We never had the pressures most families have when something like this happens, from the job or the financial worries. Jim was a free man, and he was able to stay right with me, right at Eric's bedside, practically full-time. That was so important; it made such a difference. I understood then why we were doing this business. I understood how special it really was."

Eric is today a happy, well-adjusted eight-year-old. He wears braces and uses a walker; but according to his parents, he "doesn't even know he is handicapped; we've never used that word." And the Dornan Amway business, rather than collapsing under the weight of such a traumatic year, has grown in spectacular fashion over the past few years. They are now Crown Directs. "Eric's birth defect is no longer the center of our life," they say. "The center of our life is living and getting *on* with it."

For many Amway people, the road has had a few bumpy spots, and often the very troubles they encounter give a fresh perspective on what they are doing and why they do it.

One such couple is Mickey and Dottie Hamlett, who built a Double Diamondship in North Carolina on sheer desire. Mickey was a schoolteacher who "worked this business seven nights a week for three years to be free. I don't regret one night of it," he says now. "I would shovel out henhouses seven nights a week for three years, if that's what I had to do to be free!"

On Valentine's Day in 1979, Mickey went to his physician for a routine checkup. Thirty-eight years old, he had never spent a night in a hospital in his life. The doctor told him he had a viral infection in his lungs, but thought it would get better without treatment. The next day the pain started. "I've never known pain like what I felt that day," he says. "It was like a knife in my side. I went to the hospital; they gave me two shots to stop the pain, but it didn't stop." X rays showed that Mickey had pleurisy—fluid between the linings of the lungs. He was wheeled into a hospital room, given intravenous injections, and his condition was monitored through the night.

In the early morning hours, Mickey's lung collapsed. He suffered congestive heart failure; the doctors couldn't wake him up. He was moved to an intensive-care unit, where he lay in a state of semiconsciousness for the next two days.

As Mickey's condition grew worse his doctor told Dottie, "You should call the family together; he isn't going to make it." Dottie remembers what she did when she heard that news: "I got a bag of dimes. All our Directs were there in the hospital with me, and I gave them those dimes and told them to call their distributors and ask them to pray for Mickey."

They did, and his family did, and Mickey's condition did an about-face. He regained full consciousness and began to get better. After a lengthy recovery period, which included extensive treatment at Duke University Medical Center, he returned to the full health and energy he had always known before. The experience has made him a better leader, he says; it has given him a new perspective on what life means, on how important it is to do what he does with all his heart. "I'll tell you why I didn't die," he offers. "I didn't die because God's not finished with me yet."

Despite his brush with death and despite a kidney-stone operation five months later and the birth of a child to Dottie that same year, despite all that time spent in hospital beds and waiting rooms, the Hamletts qualified as new Diamonds that year and have requalified every year since.

"Drawing circles is my therapy. When I get in front of that board, I pour my heart out. I always feel good and clean when I get through, because I know I've given it my best shot. Life can get you down if you let it, but I won't let it."

Norman Rockwell

Previous page: Norman Rockwell sketched Jay Van Andel and Rich DeVos in the 1960s, soon after Amway had begun its meteoric rise to national prominence. Van Andel *(above)* chats with workers on the powder-soap line in more recent days. *Below:* DeVos, on one of his tours of the Ada facility, is greeted by a worker.

Above: Popular radio talk-show host Larry King moderates a nation-wide broadcast of an economics discussion involving *(left to right)* Nobel Prize winner Milton Friedman, King, Rich DeVos, and Jay Van Andel. *Below:* The Home Team of executive vice-presidents at Amway: *(left to right)* Gordon Teska, Bill Halliday, Laurie Mulham, Orville Hoxie, and Robert Hunter.

Left: Former President and Mrs. Gerald R. Ford arrive at the Amway Grand Plaza Hotel.

Above: Listening to Ford's remarks are *(left to right)* Betty Van Andel, Mrs. Ford, Helen DeVos, Rich DeVos, and Jay Van Andel. *Below:* President Ford participated in the ribbon cutting ceremony opening the $60 million hotel in 1981. Van Andel and DeVos, along with Ford, hand the Grand Plaza key to hotel manager Christian F. Schunack.

Above: In 1962 this small building housed the entire Amway operation. In 1983 the company owns dozens of buildings, in various parts of North America, with over 7 million square feet under roof *(right)*. The nerve center of it all is the Center for Free Enterprise *(below)*, which anchors the sprawling Ada, Michigan, manufacturing and operations facility.

Pictured topside is the crew of the *Enterprise III*. Amway's sleek and powerful ocean-going conference ship *(below)*.

Msitslav Rostropovich, conductor of Washington's National Symphony Orchestra, visited the Ada plant for a cello concert in late 1981 *(above)*. Here Rostropovich *(right)* talks with an Amway employee who, like himself, is a Russian-born American. *Below:* An Amway-sponsored float in the 1982 Rose Bowl Parade celebrated friendship between America and the Netherlands. Riders on the float included Amway Diamond Distributors Anne and Harm Berghuis, the Netherlands' top producing distributors who now live in Canada, and Dan and Bunny Williams, Crown Ambassadors from California.

Left: Conventions and rallies are an important part of the "Amway experience." Here, in a recent Indianapolis session, Jay Van Andel speaks to a packed house.

Johnny Cash and his wife June Carter Cash *(above)* were hosted at a recent Free Enterprise Day in Dallas by Triple Diamonds Bob and Jo Crisp. *Below:* The California-based Sanborn Singers perform at corporate conventions around the country.

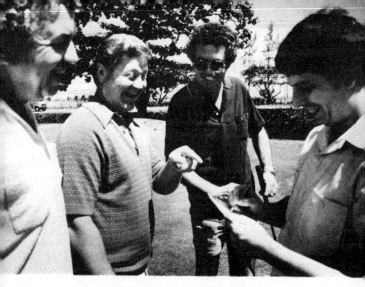

Above: Checking golf scores at Diamond Club are *(left to right)* John Hendrickson, Stan Evans, Dennis Beecher, and Jim Dornan, all Crown Directs. *Below:* It is Western Night at a 1981 Leadership Seminar, and Diamonds Jim and Bev Kinsler, from New York, whoop it up.

Above: Jerry and Cheri Meadows visit with Effie Reid, a fellow Diamond, at one of the frequent Amway weekend gatherings. *Below:* Quebec Crowns Andre and Francoise Blanchard enjoy the laughter at a banquet for Amway leaders.

Above: Another popular Amway family connection is the Crown distributorship of Bernice Hansen and her daughter and son-in-law Skip and Susan Ross. *Below:* Amway's first "second-generation" Crown distributor is Jody Victor, shown here with wife, Kathy. Jody's parents are also Crowns; the family is from Ohio.

Above: The Delisle family of San Jose, California, with three separate distributorships: *(left to right)* Double Diamonds Frank, Jr., and Barb; Crown Ambassadors Frank and Rita; Triple Diamonds Dennis and Sharon. *Below:* The entire family comes to Ada for Double Diamond Day. Here Rich DeVos gives a personal farewell to a tiny visitor outside the Center for Free Enterprise.

Amway of Canada has its own manufacturing facility, conventions, and catalog operation. Business is growing rapidly in every province. Representative of the top Canadian leaders are Crown Ambassadors Bob and Joyce Schmidt of British Columbia *(above)* and Bill and Joan Laing of Ontario *(below)*.

15 Playing for Keeps

THE DUKE OF WELLINGTON once declared that one of the greatest military victories of the British Empire was won "on the playing fields of Eton."

That famous remark expresses a view that is practically dogma among coaches and athletes: the conviction that, when a youngster plays sports, he learns more than the mechanics of a game; he learns how to win. And having learned this basic lesson, he can then go on to be a winner in all of life.

It is an appealing idea.

December 1971. Football time in the Deep South. The Gator Bowl is jammed with noisy fans, 70,000 of them. The marching bands are there, and the television cameras, and the cheerleaders— all the glamour and excitement of big-time college football. The Georgia Bulldogs are to meet the

North Carolina Tarheels in a post-season bowl game that will decide national rankings for both teams. It is an occasion and an atmosphere charged with competitive tension for each of the football players, who wait in separate locker rooms for the signal to charge onto the field. It is a moment which defines the word *pressure*.

In the North Carolina locker room, the focal point of that pressure is the quarterback, a fair-haired twenty-one-year-old English major who leads his team's attack. His name is Paul Miller. On him and his ability to execute the Carolina offense rest the hopes of tens of thousands of fans who have followed their team to Jacksonville this day. Across the stadium, in the Georgia locker room, the pressure created by an equal number of Bulldog fans falls squarely on the shoulders of a quiet young flanker back named Jimmy Shirer.

Those last few minutes of waiting stretched on a bit longer, then finally the Blue and White of Carolina and Paul Miller rushed onto the field to do combat with the Red and Black of Georgia and Jimmy Shirer. It was a viciously fought, low-scoring football game, marked by brilliant defensive play on both sides of the field, and ending in a narrow 7–3 victory for Georgia, who came into the game favored by a touchdown. The Bulldogs finished the season with eleven wins and one loss and a final ranking in the nation's Top Ten.

So Shirer and Miller walked off the field that afternoon, one in victory, the other in defeat. For both, their football careers were over. Time had come that afternoon for the two college seniors to hang up their helmets and turn to more important battles that lay ahead. Neither of them had ever heard of Amway, and in their wildest imaginations could not have dreamed that they would meet again, ten years later, both winners on the same team, on the stage of Diamond Club in Amway.

Shirer, who grew up in South Carolina and played high-school football there, had been recruited to the University of Georgia as a quarterback, was shifted to defensive back, and finally to flanker. After graduation, he followed the familiar pattern of going directly from college football to a coaching career. It was while coaching a high-school team in Opelika, Alabama, that he and his wife, Kay, began their Amway business and built it to the Emerald level. He resigned his coaching job then and became a Diamond two years later.

Miller took a different route. He came from the town of Ayder, North Carolina, where he led his high-school team to fifty-two victories in a row. Miller played five years of junior-high- and senior-high-school football without losing a game. He went to the University of North Carolina, held the starting position there for his last two seasons, and both years led the team to bowl games (the Peach Bowl against Arizona State in 1970). He met his wife, Debbie, during that time; she was a majorette at Wake Forest, and they met as blind dates at the wedding of another ballplayer. Debbie was a bridesmaid; Paul was a groomsman. Both were attractive and unattached; it was a perfect match.

After undergraduate days, Paul went straight into law school at UNC, receiving his law degree in 1976. He and Debbie had tied the marital knot in 1975 and had begun to build an Amway business. They began slowly. "At first I was scared to call people," says the man who faced 250-pound linebackers. "I was afraid of what people would think," says the man who played ball with 70,000 spectators watching. It was a weekend Amway convention, a "Dream Night" in Washington, D. C., that lit the fire for Paul and Debbie. He had not wanted to go at all, because he had an important set of law school exams the next Monday, but what he saw when he arrived in Washington made it worth the effort. "We both really saw the dream that night," he remembers. It was December 1975.

Paul began practicing law in the little town of Zebulon, North Carolina, in 1976, and he and Debbie moved to Zebulon determined not only to practice law, but also to build their new business. They did so with unusual speed: Direct in August of 1976, Pearl in 1977, Diamond in February of 1979. They have now moved from Zebulon to Raleigh, have begun a family, and are living the life of full-time Amway Diamonds, though both are barely thirty years old. Paul explains that leaving his law practice to go full-time was an easy decision: "I found I was cooped up by law practice. There is no real freedom there for a young lawyer as there is in this business. And another thing: the people we're with in this business are more relaxed, more genuine, than any other group

I've ever been around. They just *feel* good to be with! It's a real team spirit!''

For all his cool, low-key style, it is clear that fierce competitive fires burn inside Paul Miller, and perhaps it is the will to compete and win that makes his athletic background such a natural training ground for success in certain types of business. There are many such examples of blue-chip college athletes who later go on to achieve Diamond status in Amway.

Bill Wright, a Diamond in Massachusetts, was a running back at Northern Arizona University in the late 1950s. Bob Goshen, an Oklahoma Diamond, played his college football at Oklahoma State. Bill Childers, another North Carolina Diamond, played quarterback on a state championship team in high school that went undefeated for two straight seasons. Like so many high-school quarterbacks, he was recruited to play college ball, then switched to another position, defensive back.

Childers played one year at a small school, Nebraska Wesleyan, then transferred to the University of Nebraska, in the tough Big Eight Conference, to finish his career. It was after he and his wife, Hona, had settled back in North Carolina that they came into Amway and developed a Diamond-level business in the Charlotte area. The Childerses' group includes several other former ballplayers, among them past and present members of the Miami Dolphins professional football team.

Bob Kuechenberg, an All Pro defensive lineman

whom most sportswriters consider a certain Hall of Fame choice when he retires, is a newly qualified Direct in the Childerses' group, as is veteran defensive back Tim Foley. Childers understands the competitive similarities of big-time sports and the early stages of an Amway business, from his own personal experience, and is personally convinced that the transfer of a winning habit from the ball field to the business world is a natural one.

Nor is football the only sport in which such a transfer occurs. Bob Bolin played major league baseball for thirteen years, mostly with the San Francisco Giants and the Boston Red Sox. He played in two World Series, had the ninth-lowest career earned-run average (2.84) in major league history, and was considered one of the best relief pitchers in baseball in the early 1970s. But as age and a tired arm caught up with him, he diverted his competitive instincts from baseball to an Amway distributorship and became a Diamond only five years after retiring from professional sports.

In the hockey world, there is no greater legend than that of Gordie Howe. The great forward played more seasons than anyone in the history of the National Hockey League, scored more points, made more goals, had more assists than anyone else ever has. He was the league's Most Valuable Player more times (six) than anyone in history and won the league scoring title more times than anyone else ever has. When time came for the mythical Howe to hang up his stick, in late 1980, he became an Amway distributor with his wife,

Colleen, and leads a Direct Distributorship from his home near Hartford, Connecticut.

Every sport has its heroes, and probably the biggest name in America in the sport of lacrosse is that of Buddy Beardmore. For many years he coached at the University of Maryland, building its team into a lacrosse powerhouse. In eleven seasons, he won two national championships, finished second in the nation four other times, won eight championships in the Atlantic Coast Conference, and went to the NCAA playoffs a record nine straight years. During that time he coached more than forty All-American lacrosse players. The Washington, D. C., sportswriters called him "the Legend," and one analyst declared him "a genius, an innovator, one of the most successful coaches the sport has ever known."

But Beardmore is also a successful Amway distributor, a Pearl, and in early 1981 left his hard-won perch atop the world of collegiate lacrosse to pursue his business full-time.

Success, it seems, is contagious. It shifts readily from the football field and baseball diamond to the living rooms and dens and meeting places where the Amway business is done. Athletic success and Amway success have some things in common: a willingness to do whatever is necessary to win, an ability to survive the reverses, to reject the momentary defeats, to stay in the game until the victory is achieved.

No one in Amway understands those principles

better than Henry Crosby. He was a tough, scrappy football player who became an Amway Diamond on sheer drive and determination. Crosby played college ball at the University of South Carolina. He had been a running back in high school, but seemed too small to make it in that position—or any other—at a major college. When he arrived on campus in 1958, he stood only 5'8" and weighed 150 pounds.

Crosby made the team sheerly on the strength of his desire and his fighting spirit. "I was small," he concedes, "but there was no 'quit' in me. They had me practicing at linebacker during my sophomore year, and I would get so beat up I could barely get out of bed. But nothing was going to make me quit. I needed that football scholarship to get through college; I simply couldn't afford it any other way. So I stuck it out." As a senior, not only was Crosby still surviving, but he was on the first team on both offense and defense. "LSU ran a big two hundred eighty-five-pound tackle at me, one-on-one, all day long. They thought they would run the ball at the little man," he recalls of that memorable game. "I was scared to death at first, but I just stuck my nose in there, and after the first few plays I was enjoying it."

When Crosby started his Amway distributorship, he "stuck his nose in there" in the same straightforward fashion. After college, he married Pat, herself a fine athlete from a sports-oriented family (her father had been an All-American football player; her brother played at Duke) and moved to Alabama to attend dental school. After that came a tour of duty in the Air Force, then the Crosbys returned to South Carolina to begin a dental practice. It was an old dental school buddy, Tom Payne, who called the Crosbys one day to invite them to see a new business he was in.

"We drove nine hundred miles to Alabama, purely out of respect for Tom and Carolyn, and plain old curiosity, to see this business," Pat remembers. Henry at first recoiled from the idea of joining Amway, but Pat responded positively: "Henry's dental practice was consuming him; he was working so hard. I wanted him to be able to relax a little—to be able to go duck hunting when he felt like it." Eventually Henry decided to try it. They would give it 100-percent effort for one year, he said, and then take a hard look and see what they thought of it. During that one year it would be all or nothing, he declared. Once they began, for the next year, they would refuse even to think about quitting.

So with that strategy, they became Amway distributors. "There was no 'quit' in me," Crosby had said of his football days, and the same was true of him in Amway. A 150-pound defensive back who enjoys a head-butting contest with a 285-pound offensive lineman is not likely to be intimidated by a box of soap. The Crosbys did stay that first year and every year thereafter and today lead an active, growing Amway organization of their own. It is another example of a winner on the football field becoming a winner in another, more profitable arena.

To Henry Crosby, success in Amway was a matter of being willing to stick his nose in. That was something he had learned to do, long ago, on a South Carolina football field.

16 Jumping Off the Pedestal

A MARTIAN getting a first look at Planet Earth might well conclude that, on this strange planet, the local gods wear uniforms with numbers on their backs. Large crowds of faithful worshipers gather regularly in places called stadiums or coliseums, to practice a passionate secular religion called Spectator Sports.

Athletes in contemporary America are lionized, pampered, envied, romanticized—yes, even worshiped—by a society hungry for heroes. Any little boy who has ever thrown a pass or canned a jump shot or stolen second base has, at one time or another, enjoyed his own fantasies of making it as a big-time athlete. The tallest and most glittering pedestals in contemporary America are occupied by professional athletes. They travel first-class, stay in the best hotels, eat the best steaks, have their bodies kneaded and rubbed by the most talented masseurs, and enjoy the adulation of an adoring public. Their names and faces fill the newspapers and airwaves, and they are cheered regularly by thousands of fans who pay good money to watch them play a game they enjoy; with all this, they receive six-figure salaries. Who would trade that life for any conceivable alternative?

Dave Taylor would.

Dave Taylor—number 64—offensive left tackle for the NFL Baltimore Colts. A man who spent a lifetime learning to push other giants around on a 100-yard football field, who took a magnificent God-given body plus years of hard work to make it to the starting roster of a professional football team. Taylor was living what so many people regard as the quintessential American Dream, the glamorous life and big bucks of the pro athlete. But for Dave Taylor, as for so many of his colleagues in major-league sports, life in the fast lane wasn't what it was cracked up to be. He began to look for an alternative.

"Ever since I was a kid," Taylor remembers, "I've always wanted to be somebody. The Good Lord endowed me with a big body—over ten pounds when I was born. I worked at football. To be a pro football player was an obsession within me. I ate it, slept it, and dreamed it. I became good at knocking people's heads off. I loved going out there and showing people what an animal I was. When I played in college, I had a couple of knee operations, and a doctor told me I should quit. He said if I didn't, there was a danger of my eventually becoming a cripple. But I refused to listen. I wasn't going to let him take that dream away from me."

After a college career at a small North Carolina school, Catawba College, Taylor was drafted by the Colts and made the team as a rookie in 1976. He grew to his present size, 6'3" and 260 pounds, and became a regular member of the offensive and special-teams units for the next four seasons. He had a couple of cars, a house, and the life-style that goes along with it. His last contract with the Colts was a multiyear deal for $480,000. That was the good news. The bad news was that none of it added up to the good life for him and his wife, Lorna. She wanted him to get out of football: "I was tired of packing icepacks for him every night, tired of watching him unable to get out of bed for two days after every game. I was tired of the stress, the negative environment he was part of. He had had two knee operations, a cracked bone in his back, torn ligaments, and a pinched nerve in his neck that would sometimes make his right arm go dead."

Taylor's various aches and pains and the stress of the hypercompetitive atmosphere, gradually took its toll. "I felt good about what I had achieved, and I was making a good living," he explains. "But I wasn't a husband to my wife. I wasn't a father to my children. I was beginning to drink more because I was always uptight. The game of football is a beautiful game, but at that level it's just a job. I played hurt. I played when I knew it was bad for me. Finally, I realized: *Taylor, you're just a slab of meat!*

"After four years in the NFL, I woke up one morning and saw the lines in my face. I sounded like a one-man band getting out of bed. My bones all popped and cracked. It scared me. I had counted on football being the source of my personal financial freedom, and I saw it wasn't going to happen. I looked at all the old retired football players, looked at their life-styles. I knew I didn't want to be there ten or fifteen years down the road. I had given fifteen years of my life to a sport so that I could be personally free, and I saw it just wasn't going to happen. Even if I stayed with it for several more years, I saw I couldn't achieve long-range personal freedom through that job."

That realization coincided with the Taylors' introduction to Amway. A friend invited them to a meeting to see the Amway Plan. Lorna looked around the room that night and, as she tells it, immediately saw an environment she wanted to join. The people were well dressed. There was no liquor, no bad language. The atmosphere was wholesome and oriented toward both members of the husband-wife couples. "Deep down," she thought, "that's how I want us to be."

They joined and for about ten months made only a limited commitment to building a business. Almost nothing happened. But in early 1978, things began to move as Taylor developed a more and more aggressive approach. The word spread among his teammates that he was taking his new soap business seriously, and predictably, the locker-room jibes increased. "I had to eat a little crow for a while," he admits. "I'd go into the locker room and somebody would call me 'Soapy.' I was introduced to the rookies that year as 'Mr. Amway.' They'd ask me, 'Been knocking on any doors lately, Soapy?' When I came into the locker room one day, two or three guys jumped on a bench and began singing 'God Bless America!' I just jumped on a stool and sang it with them, as loud as I could. They weren't bad guys; they just didn't understand what I was doing. Besides, I didn't care what they thought, because I had a dream. My dream was to be free."

And that dream came true. The Taylors showed the Plan night after night, to all kinds of people. Within three years the business was so large that the football income became dispensable, and Number Sixty-four decided the time had come to hang up the jersey. He went to the stadium that day, in late 1979, went around the locker room shaking hands with his teammates, telling them goodbye. Some of them tried to talk him out of his decision, arguing that he couldn't possibly give up the salary, insisting that he would eventually regret it. He never even hesitated. "I packed my bag and walked out that locker room for the last time. I got in my little 280Z and did a doughnut in that parking lot. When I looked back in the rearview mirror and realized I didn't have to go back, it was worth every moment, every circle, every tear, every no-show!

"This business showed me a whole new way of life," he says now, as a Diamond Direct. "The money was the hook for me. That's why I started. But after I got in, I found not just money but love. I found friends. I found people I could cry with. I found out what real giving and real humility was all about. This business made a winner out of me. It took a boy with a two-hundred-and-sixty-pound body and made him grow up."

Lorna agrees. "It's true," she says. "Dave had a big ego from being a football player and being on a pedestal, but he was willing to take his ego off and lay it aside and learn to do this business. It takes a real man to do that."

17 Artiste

THERE IS A WAY to make a living that is even more glamorous than professional athletics: a career in the performing arts. It has the same glitter and dazzle, without the necessity of having one's body assaulted by a fellow performer. No cracked bones and torn ligaments, no weekly mangling on Sunday afternoon, but still the chance to make a good living by performing in front of all those people! All that applause! All those ego strokes! What could be more glamorous than a career in the performing arts?

In California, at opposite ends of the state, live two Amway couples who moved West to pursue careers in performance. In southern California, home of show biz, Hollywood, the motion picture industry, and all the razzmatazz that goes with it, one finds Ron and Dinah Stokes. And in northern California, home of hot tubs, Stanford University, the San Francisco Opera Company, and the celebrated Bay Area sophistication, one finds Ben and Nancy Dominitz. Both couples seem entirely at home in their chosen environments.

Ron and Dinah Stokes are Double Diamonds, for whom busy careers in show business have gradually given way to heavier involvement in a growing Amway distributorship. He is from the Midwest—Omaha, to be exact, but that was long ago. He is in his mid-forties, still young looking, still nimble when he puts on his dancing shoes. His life story is straight out of the fan magazines: always wanted to be an actor, always loved to make people laugh, finally escaped Nebraska for the Promised Land of southern Cal. He went to San Jose State University to major in speech and drama, then right down the coast to Los Angeles to try to make a living as an actor.

That is a familiar story, but Ron was one of the few who made it. He did repertory theater, summer stock, whatever. He hired an agent. He did television shows—over one hundred of them—and small parts in movies. He did commercials. He was a hard-working actor who stayed busy and made a lot of money and was proud of his craft.

After eight years in Los Angeles, he met Dinah, herself an actress and a native of Los Angeles. They met while playing in a production of *Barefoot in the Park* at the Santa Monica Community Theater, and were married in 1970. A few months later they heard about Amway. Ron tells it: "I had worked with this woman on some TV commercials, and she called one day and asked if I would like to make some extra money. She wanted me to come over and look at a presentation of some kind. I was very skeptical, and showed it. 'Leave your checkbook at home and come take a look,' she said. So we did. We went to her home; six or eight couples were there. A fellow named Ben Cooper showed the Plan. That's how it all started." (Cooper, himself a veteran Hollywood actor, is now also a Diamond.)

They went home that night and talked it over. Ron: "You want to do it?" Dinah: "I don't know. You want to do it?" And in that emphatic fashion, they decided to do it.

Predictably, many of the people whom they sponsored into the business worked in the entertainment industry, especially in the first few years. They built to Direct Distributor quickly, progressed during the next few years to Diamond and Double Diamond, and consider themselves to be still in the "early growth" stage of what is already a large distributorship. Ron, who struggled through the lean years so common for young actors, describes the financial payoffs from Amway as "helping people get rid of the economic cancer that eats them alive." He remembers his own hand-to-mouth years: "I've lived from week to week. I've lived in a theater basement with the windows out, sleeping on an old cot. That's not a hard-luck story—just a fact. I remember calling my mom and asking her to send me five dollars. I know what it's like to be broke. It's like an economic cancer that keeps people from utilizing the talent they have.''

Dinah talks about the personal changes she has experienced in Amway. She has become more patient, she says, more tolerant, more willing to understand other people and deal with them effectively. "And it has made me more analytical about my own behavior as well," she says. "I want to be able to look in the mirror and feel that I have really done a good job. I love the recognition I get in this business, and I want to know that I have really earned it."

They are an attractive couple. It is easy to imagine them on stage, in the spotlight, a part of the glitter and glamour of show business. "Glamour?" Ron asks. "Glamour? To a professional actor, acting is just a job. If you want to see glamour, get in the Amway business! That's where the glamour is!"

A few hundred miles up the coast, there is a different California. And in the northern California world of Ben and Nancy Dominitz, one finds a different glamour. It is a world of performance, but a different kind of performance, in which the artist is more likely to wear white tie and tails than a cowboy suit, where one competent cellist is more highly valued than a dozen stand-up comics. In the Dominitz world, the heroes' names are not Fonda, Streisand, or Burt Reynolds—but Bernstein, Sills, and Itzhak Perlman.

Ben Dominitz knew he would be a performer

from the age of seven, when he heard his first violin concerto on a radio in his home in Tel Aviv. His parents were not musicians themselves, but they recognized the talent of their precocious son and moved from their home in Israel to enable him to study at The Juilliard School of music in New York City in 1963. He was only thirteen years old, a promising young violinist with a full scholarship to study with the world-famous Juilliard faculty. After five years there, he moved on to the University of Cincinnati, to the Conservatory of Music. There he met Nancy, a voice major from Ohio, and the two married, moving soon afterward to the Indiana University School of Music for more graduate study.

"We love music," Ben says in what qualifies as classic understatement. "In graduate school, however, we became a bit disillusioned with the politics of the music world. We love music, but not the very small music world. I saw one of my favorite professors at Cincinnati, a genuinely brilliant musician, reduced to begging to keep his job because he didn't fit well into the politics of the conservatory. I think that example, more than any other single factor, started us looking for some source of income outside music."

They saw a small ad on a bulletin board at the university, answered it, and in that rather unpromising way came into the business. "We had never heard of Amway, so we had no hangups whatever. We saw the potential immediately; but to be honest, we struggled for a while before we really made any progress at all. It was almost three years before we began to have an inkling of what this business was all about."

In 1975, Ben received the offer that brought him and Nancy to California; he was asked to play first violin in the Sacramento Symphony Orchestra and to lead the Sacramento Symphony String Quartet. The challenge of that new position so occupied him that for the first seven months in California, the Dominitzes completely ignored their small Amway business, and by the time they turned their attention back to it, there was very little business left.

But in 1976 they resumed their Amway activity, this time with a fresh enthusiasm, and now things fell into place. They broke as Directs four months later and since then have achieved new pin levels with a steady beat: Direct in 1976; Ruby in 1977; Pearl in 1978; Emerald in 1979; Diamond in 1980. Their distributorship is drawn from middle- and upper-middle-class suburbanites ("Only because there aren't very many blue-collar workers around here"), almost entirely within 150 miles of Sacramento. They refer to the people they sponsor as their "Amway family," and they are proud of its ethnic and demographic diversity.

Ben is very active as a professional musician, although he no longer plays with the Sacramento Symphony. He confesses to having "an allergy" to a nine-to-five job, even in music, and prefers a more independent situation. Early in 1982, for example, he conducted two performances of the opera *Hansel and Gretel* with the Stockton Opera Company. And Nancy, who no longer pursues a performing career, seems to have found her *métier* in the Amway business. "She is a fantastic businesswoman," Ben declares. "She has such great skill with people, and she is absolutely talented in the administration of our business."

The Dominitzes' background is serious music; the Stokeses' is show biz. For both of them, the future is brighter than a giant bank of klieg lights. The curtain is up. The applause has already begun. Nothing makes a performer happier than that.

18 Police Story

EVERYONE ENJOYS a police story.

Amway lore includes several good ones. Is it merely a coincidence, or is there something about police work that prepares a man for extraordinary achievement in a business such as Amway?

Charlie Marsh was Amway's first Crown, and for years one of its best-known speakers and motivators. He came to the business from the streets of Rome, New York, where for nine years he wore a badge and patrolled a beat. Another "first" was achieved by policeman Dick Marks, of Winnipeg's finest, who became the original Crown Ambassador in 1978. And the first black Diamond Direct, George Halsey, was a cop, too, from Greensboro, North Carolina.

Amway people are accustomed to hearing police stories with happy endings—stories that end with rewards that are more substantial than merely the satisfaction of a "good" arrest.

There's another police story making the rounds recently, this one from a city with a rather more violent reputation than Winnipeg, Greensboro, or upstate New York: Chicago, a city that takes its crime—and its cops—seriously. When a man wears a badge in downtown Chicago, he rarely enjoys a relaxed day helping little old ladies cross the street. He expects to be challenged from time to time.

Lee Besser was always up to the challenge.

He was a city kid who grew up on the Chicago streets. He dropped out of high school because he found it boring, and worked at odd jobs—construction, factory line, pizza joint, whatever brought a little money. That was in the late 1960s, and healthy young men without college deferments became prime targets for the military draft as Vietnam began to heat up. Besser's number came up, and in the course of two Vietnam tours of duty as a combat door-gunner, he began to develop as an achiever and a leader. He came home as a sergeant, twenty-six years old and ready for something more demanding than the life of a handyman.

He became a cop. In 1970 he entered the Chicago Police Academy and went into the force. "It was a tough job, but I was young and idealistic, and at first I liked it a lot. I wasn't married at the time, and I really enjoyed police work. I felt I was doing something worthwhile with my life. But it grinds you down after a few years. I got into a rut. I was a good copper, but it got to be just a job, a grind.''

There was a bar next door to the precinct station where Besser worked, and like many of his fellow officers, he spent many of his off-duty hours there. "It was a hole-in-the-wall place, really," he remembers. "But there were always thirty or forty cops there. I would drop in after work, put a five-dollar bill down, and stay there for a couple of hours 'til I drank it up. We'd tell cop stories and kind of unwind before we went home."

It was at another bar that Besser met a woman who worked at a bank nearby. Her name was Jane, and after four years of an on-and-off relationship, they married. "Just like that," she remembers, "by a justice of the peace in downtown Chicago. We just *did* it." The marriage soon settled into an uninspiring routine. He worked, she worked, but still there seemed never to be enough money. "At the end of every month," Jane recalls, "we'd get into a fight over the money. We never had enough for a vacation or to go out to eat. My dream was someday not to have any outstanding bills. That's all. Or maybe to have a set of furniture that matched."

Besser wanted kids, but not on a police salary. "I loved kids," he says. "I always did. I really wanted a houseful of them, but I wanted a good life for them. I was thirty-three years old, and still no kids. But when I looked around me on the force, I saw other cops killing themselves to pay the bills. They had kids and never saw them; they were putting in sixty to eighty hours a week to support the kids and never had time to be with them. I didn't want that."

Then along came Amway. Jane saw it first. The union steward where she worked asked her one day if she was interested in making more money. Of course she was. "What is it?" she asked, and was told to come with him to a meeting the next Friday and take a look for herself.

She went. "I sat in that room and got so excited! I saw it as a great opportunity immediately. I knew Lee and I could do it. I knew if the two of us got together on this thing, nothing on earth could keep us from doing it." She went home, eager to tell her husband about Amway. He had been working that night and came home later than expected. She waited about three hours, until he finally arrived, and she explained it all to him.

"Lee had been out with his police friends and was a little ripped," she tells. "I showed him the circles. He got mad. We fought. We screamed and fought for three days. I wanted him to go with me to a meeting and see it for himself, and he wanted nothing to do with it. He finally agreed to go, just once. So we went. There were about a hundred people there. I was scared he wouldn't even consider it. He sat there and listened, and when it was over, he simply said, 'I can do that.' That's all there was to it."

They never looked back. From that first night, Lee and Jane Besser made an all-out assault on their new challenge. "I was ready for it," Lee says. "I was looking for a better life than what I had. I wanted more out of life, and I was willing to work for it; I just didn't know how to go about it. I was tired of having to call in on the radio to get permission to eat lunch. I was tired of working so hard when nobody cared. When Amway came along, I was ready."

From the day they signed the Amway application, Besser went six months without taking a drink. "I wanted this thing so badly," he explains, "that I'd have worn a dress if I had to! Whatever it took, that's what I was going to do!" The Bessers started working together, started spending time together, planning their schedules together. They had ten meetings in a row when nobody joined, tried to sponsor almost a hundred people without success. "Our dream was so strong, there was nothing going to stop us." And then, in the next twenty days, after weeks of total frustration, they sponsored six new distributors, all of whom are still successful distributors today. Those six formed the nucleus of what would become a Diamond Direct distributorship within four years.

That distributorship includes many of Lee's fellow police officers, one of whom is an Emerald, another a Pearl. It includes a Direct whom Jane prospected on the subway on the way to work. It includes a friend who worked for fourteen years as a meat cutter before retiring as a Pearl. And it includes some of Lee's old acquaintances from the other side of the law as well. "Yeah, I've had several of those," he says. "I'll have guys come up to me at meetings and say 'Hey remember me, you pinched me for auto theft.' 'Hey, remember me, I'm so-and-so; you grabbed me on a larceny thing.' I was called to a really rough section one night to throw some bikers out of a bar. They were all done up in their leather jackets and all that. I went in to take care of the disturbance, and one of the bikers said to me, 'Hey, I sold a gallon drum of LOC yesterday!' I didn't know the guy, of course, but he obviously had seen me at a meeting somewhere."

Lots of things have changed for the Bessers. He is no longer a policeman, having resigned from the force to work his Amway business full-time. Jane no longer works outside the home; she now has the children they've always wanted; *four* children within four years, in fact. Their home is a farmhouse now, replacing the city apartment, with a vacation home in Wisconsin to go along with it. And there is security that was absent before. "One of the best things about this business to me is the knowledge that if I die, Jane gets more than a lousy pension or an insurance policy from the city of Chicago."

And there are other, smaller, changes: "Like my phone book, for instance. It has millionaires in it now, not just hoods and cops. Four years ago I didn't have a prospect list; I had a suspect list. You know, 'This guy's a junkie; this guy's a shoplifter.' Now it's, 'This guy's a Diamond; this guy's a Pearl!' "

19 Changed Lives

IT IS STARTLING to hear people say that a soap business has changed their lives.

That language seems rather overdone for something so mundane as a part-time business. One's life is changed by the monumental events: by marriage, by religious conversion, by education, by personal tragedy or achievement on a grand scale. But by an Amway distributorship?

Yet that phrase is heard frequently, everywhere Amway people gather to tell their stories, and the honest observer must conclude, when he has all the facts, that they are right. Their lives *have* been changed, in positive directions, often with permanent results.

The most obvious changes are those that accompany increased income. Amway is a business venture for individuals. The reason people get involved is to earn money, and Amway's track record shows that many of them do make money, sometimes large amounts of it. That money brings new things into their lives and alters the way they live. These are the most direct and most obvious ways in which people's lives are changed by Amway.

The case of Gary and Diane Reasons is an example of this process. They grew up in the small town of Eldorado, in downstate Illinois. They met on the first day of school as high-school sophomores; it was a small-town courtship of charming simplicity, the kind one rarely sees today. "I guess we fell in love that first day," Diane reflects. "Gary always seemed different. He didn't seem to fit that little town. He was a big dreamer. He is the only person, to this day, I've ever dated, the only boy I've ever even had a Coke with." They eloped when Gary was eighteen and Diane was seventeen, driving across the state line into Kentucky to be married at midnight by a justice of the peace.

Gary got a job at Western Auto; Diane got pregnant; it must have seemed that whatever dreams they had would be buried in the narrow world of Eldorado. But the Reasons did not give up so easily. They saved a bit of money and left, with their child, for Southern Illinois University, in Carbondale. Gary entered engineering school; Diane paid the rent with a $198-per-month job as a typist. After college came a job offer at McDonnell-Douglas, in Saint Louis. Gary took the position, but it was such humdrum office work and paid so little, that he left it for a direct-sales job with a vacuum-cleaner company, which in turn took him to Cincinnati.

Within a year, the Reasons were broke. Their vacuum-cleaner business in Cincinnati had failed, a victim of bad loans and the collapse of the parent company. They moved back to Saint Louis, bitterly disillusioned, to start over again. Diane had to return to work. Gary found a new position, plus a second, part-time job, to try to pay off old bills. He returned to college, two nights a week, to improve his value in the job market. And on top of it all, he constantly looked for extra income opportunities. "I always thought something would come along to help us break out," he declares. "I was *hungry* when Amway came."

That hunger propelled the Reasons' distributorship to Diamond status, and along the way they have acquired the usual assortment of expensive possessions that fit a genuinely luxurious life-style. Such changes of a material nature are to be expected whenever one's income increases dramatically, whatever the business that produces that increase. But there are other, more profound ways in which the Reasons are different: changes that they attribute not just to money, but specifically to the special flavor of the Amway experience.

"We had our faith in people restored," Diane puts it simply. "When we got involved, we saw love; we felt love. It made us different." Gary says their new Amway friends were a big part of the change: "Before Amway, we could count our close friends on one hand. There were very few people at

that time I could have called and asked for help
and gotten it. At our first rally, I heard a guy say,
'If there were no money in Amway, I would still do
this for friendship.' I looked at Diane and told her,
'*That* I don't believe!' Now I understand. Amway
gave me a new faith in other people. I had been
burned, and I was bitter. Amway brought me out
of that. I believe I could call any one of thousands
of other distributors and say, 'Hey, I need you,'
and that person would be there—no questions
asked. How can you put a price on that?''

The changes Robert Echols made as a result of
Amway were of a more visible sort. He was an
East Texas roughneck who grew up "fightin' and
cussin' and carryin' on" in the best tradition of the
oil fields. He grew up poor. He and his father,
"ate a lot of squirrel meat we shot," and Robert
barely made it through high school, leaving a trail
of bad grades and bad-conduct reports behind
him.

He worked at dozens of jobs: ran a jackhammer
on a highway construction gang, rode broncos and
bulls in the rodeo, was a carpenter, a welder,
worked on oil rigs in the Gulf of Mexico, where on
one occasion he recalls "riding out a 125-mile-
per-hour hurricane." (Was he frightened? "Nah,
not really. Ninety percent of the things you worry
about never happen, and the other ten percent you
can't do nothin' about anyway.") Echols was
working as a welder when he was invited to his
first Amway meeting. "It was a bunch of dignified

folks at a bank. The sole was loose on my left shoe. A fellow named Dan Williams gave the Plan, and he really was impressive, so I got in immediately.''

That night Robert Echols' whole approach to life began to change. "When I got into this business, I knew I had to make some changes. I wanted it badly, so I changed. I made a pledge to myself: 'Echols, from now on, no more fighting and very little cussing,' and I stuck to it. I went out and bought some teeth right away. I bought a suit and a shirt to go with those teeth. I owed money to just about everybody in town, and I started paying off.''

He had something to pay off with: his Amway business earned $41,000 for him the first full year and has gone up from there. And Echols himself has changed from the roughneck of those days; he is more comfortable in a three-piece suit than a carpenter's bib and is today every inch the poised, self-confident business executive. He still enjoys telling stories from the good-old-bad-old days, though, and there is just enough of the old Echols style to convince the listener that this man really *has* changed.

Other examples of Amway's tendency to pro-duce permanent changes are less dramatic, but no less remarkable. George Rudd worked for twenty years as a linotype operator for a Saskatoon daily newspaper. He was quiet, withdrawn, ideally suited to a job that requires little interaction with other people. But today he is a Diamond and conducts group meetings regularly with crowds of over a thousand people. At such meetings he talks to more people in a single night than in six months at his former job.

Few Amway leaders demonstrate that type of changed status more graphically than Dexter and Birdie Yeager, North Carolina Crowns who before Amway earned ninety-five dollars a week working for a brewery in upstate New York. The Yeagers' Amway success has propelled them into a position of influence and importance. They hobnob with famous and powerful people, have attended political briefing sessions at the White House, and once appeared as celebrity-guest cohosts of "Good Morning Carolina," a popular Charlotte television talk show.

"There is no gain without pain," says an old bit of folk wisdom. Certainly the dramatic changes that occur in the lives of profitable Amway distributors do not come without a price. Amway people who make great gains almost always do so as a result of great sacrifice. They speak of "paying the price." They spend sleepless nights driving home from meetings, give up bowling leagues and summer softball teams, swear off their bridge clubs and tailgate parties on Saturday afternoons —all to wedge out the time required to build their new businesses.

"Paying the price" for David Hamby meant putting away his golf clubs for a few years. Golf is a sport that claims many devoted players, but with Hamby it was a pursuit that bordered on obsession. Before he and his wife, Mary, were wed, he specifically and emphatically declared his golf days off limits to her. If marriage meant less golf, he told her, he would prefer to stay single!

Hamby was an administrator at the University of South Carolina—and a scratch golfer—when he and Mary decided to become Amway distributors. He knew himself well enough to realize that there was no time for golf and Amway success on the scale he dreamed of it, so he stashed his golf clubs. It must have been an act as painful as it would be for Farrah Fawcett to shave her head. But his withdrawal pains eventually subsided, and he and Mary built a Diamond business. Today he is retired from administrative work and has the time, money, and freedom to tee it up whenever and wherever the mood strikes.

Donald Aultman was a college professor in Tennessee who paid a different kind of price. He and his wife, Winona, had begun a business while he taught undergraduate psychology students. They became increasingly convinced that Amway offered the mid-life career shift they were seeking— so convinced that they decided to take a full year's leave of absence from his teaching post, in order to develop their business more rapidly. That would mean living for a year off savings and investment money, and that is the price they agreed to pay.

They knew exactly what they were doing. By the end of that year, the Aultmans were earning far more money from Amway than his teaching salary and had established the base for the Diamondship that provides what is now a genuinely luxurious life-style in a posh Atlanta suburb.

Amway people who are determined to pay the necessary price for a positive life change do so in many forms. Their stories are replete with accounts of sacrifice, small and large, which make the whole scenario of Amway success a more believable one. It is impossible, even in Amway, to get something for nothing. The intelligent man or woman who seeks a changed life-style expects to do difficult things in exchange for it.

Barry Land understood and embraced that principle.

He was thirty-seven years old when he died, leaving to his wife, Carol, and his two young children the security of a Diamondship distributorship. Barry was a tough, pragmatic former Marine officer. He had been a helicopter pilot in Vietnam and was sponsored into Amway while still on active duty in the Marine Corps. He was one of those men who refused to quit when things were discouraging; he showed the Plan to fifty-six people, in his first three months in the business, without sponsoring anyone.

But his natural grit and hard work paid off, and he and Carol had put the hard times well behind them, having built a lucrative Diamond business in Mississippi, at the time he learned he had cancer of the liver. By the time the diagnosis was made, the disease was already severe; he began losing weight and strength rapidly. His doctor told him he had maybe three months to live. It was July, 1980.

Most men, upon receiving that grim news, would have closed up the Amway shop and turned their attention to themselves. But not Barry Land. He was determined to leave to his family the largest, most solid business possible and to leave to his distributors a sturdy organization in which to work. So rather than backing off his Amway schedule, he increased the pace. He would take a full dose of chemotherapy in the afternoon, show the Plan that night, conduct a "Night Owl" training session until midnight, then go to a restaurant and counsel distributors until the wee hours. He would get up to see the kids off to school the next morning, then start to work again. He knew there was a price to pay for his family's future, and he was willing to pay it.

"He built this business when he didn't feel like it," Carol emphasizes.

By late October he was slipping. He had lost sixty pounds in two months. He was hospitalized in Jackson and called Kay Fletcher, a fellow Diamond and close friend, to his bedside. He could barely speak. When he did, it was not to make small talk or to discuss his condition, but to urge Kay to help his distributors, to encourage them and give them moral support in Barry's absence. "I don't think I'm coming out of this bed, Kay," he whispered. "For the next few months, it's going to be hard on my people. Will you spend some time with them? Don't let them get discouraged, help them if you can. . . ." Even from his hospital bed, Barry Land was still building a dream.

That was Saturday, November 8, 1980. On the next Tuesday, on his thirteenth wedding anniversary, he died.

"He was a winner," declares Carol. "He had a special sense of urgency about him." Barry Land was one of those men who never quit doing whatever it took to make things better for the people he loved.

20 Down on the Farm

THERE IS AN old saying that all good farmers live poor and die rich. It costs so much to run a farm, to acquire land and new machinery, that every available dollar must be poured back into the operation, leaving little for frills and frivolity. But after forty years of such skimping, the mortgages finally get paid and the net worth of the farm has escalated into big value. So the good farmer lives poor and dies rich.

That prospect is not too exciting to the ordinary youngster growing up on a farm, especially not these days, and ambitious young men and women, some of them with many generations of farmers in their backgrounds, leave the farm to go off to college and never return.

Not Mel and Bea Behnke.

They both grew up on farms—he in Kansas, she in Nebraska—and went away to college. They met while attending McPherson College, in Kansas, and from the very first they intended to return to the farm, not to flee from it. "I loved the farm," Mel says. "I always did. I always had definite goals about what I wanted to accomplish in life, but they always involved farming. And at the age of thirty-one, when I first saw Amway, I was ahead of schedule toward achieving them."

He started early. When he was ten years old, Mel's father gave him a calf. He spent $30 on feed to fatten the calf, sold it for $80, and had $50 profit. That was the start. He then took the $50 and bought five more little calves for ten dollars each, bought more feed on credit, and began the process again. One of that batch went for $274, two years later. His father allowed him to miss school to attend cattle sales, and by the time he was sixteen years old, he had put over a thousand dollars in a savings account and was building a sizable herd. He loved it.

It was not surprising, then, that after one year in college, Mel Behnke was ready to take his bride back home to Bushton, Kansas, and get started on his own. "I was only making Cs anyway and really didn't study very much to get the Cs. I knew enough from practical experience on the farm to make passing grades, and that's what I made. I finally decided to drop out of college and get to work."

For the next ten years they farmed and did well. They had pigs, cattle, and grain. It was not easy work; making a living on a farm never is. The winters were long and often bitterly cold on the Kansas plains. One winter the temperatures skidded down to twenty to thirty degrees below zero, and the Behnkes lost many of their little pigs to the cold. They had no insulation in their livestock buildings, and the youngest pigs could not survive the freezing temperatures. Bea remembers Mel bringing many of them into the house, setting up rows of little cardboard boxes around the kitchen stove, to keep the pigs warm during the cold snap.

Much as they enjoyed the farming life, the Behnkes were too practical not to worry about the lack of security that goes along with it. "In farming," Mel explains, "every year I had to risk my entire net worth just to make a profit. And the profit then went right back into the farm." And Bea was concerned about what might occur if a disabling accident—or worse—should happen to Mel. "I had an automobile accident and broke a hip," she recalls. "I realized how devastating that would have been if it had been Mel, rather than me. At about the same time, Mel's father was killed in an accident. That was a real blow, and it reminded me that if something happened to Mel, I had absolutely no way to produce income on my own. So I was making plans to return to college, part-time, to finish my teaching degree. I didn't really *want* to teach, but I didn't know anything else."

So the timing was right when a relative drove up from Texas to show them the Amway Plan. That night, in their farmhouse, he drew the circles for them on a piece of cardboard. They got in. Mel sat there and looked at the circles and concluded that being a Direct Distributor could earn $100,000 for him over a lifetime: "In those days, you could buy a quarter of land for $50,000. I figured going Direct was worth $100,000. When I thought about how hard I'd have to work on the farm to buy two quarters of land, I knew this thing was worth giving a try."

Bea had simpler thoughts: "My first goal was to get rid of the pigs; my second goal was to get rid of the cows!"

One sobering reality must be injected here: Bushton, Kansas. To build an Amway business that buys that quarter of land or gets rid of those pigs, there must be lots of people sponsored. People is something Bushton does not have a lot of. It lies right in the geographic center of the state of Kansas. Bushton is not your basic metropolitan hub. It says something about Bushton's isolation that it is most frequently described as being "near" something called Great Bend, Kansas. Dodge City is one hundred miles away. Bushton is not exactly Boston. Bushton is not Baltimore. It's not even Boise, for heaven's sake!

Oh, well. If one is a farmer, one sponsors a farmer, and farmers in Bushton are like muggers in Central Park: there are plenty of them. Mel began by sharing the business with his neighbor, another farmer, named Beneke. "We both fed hogs; we both fed cattle; we both had the same kind of tractor." The Benekes got in. Next they shared it with Mel's sister and her husband, Glenn and Marilyn Wilkens. They were also farmers, and they also got in. Then another farming couple nearby signed up, and they were off and running. Mel and Bea's sponsors were 500 miles away, so they immediately began holding their own sponsoring meetings. "We had to," Mel explains. "My first few times giving the Plan, it was not very good. I spoke for about five minutes, and it was not very good."

No matter. The Behnkes' Amway business took off like—well, like a greased pig. They attended their first rally in Texas, driving all Friday night to get there and all Saturday night to get back. That was in November, their seventh month in the business, and by January they had broken as Silver Producers with a PV level of 8100. Two of their distributors followed them, one breaking over in March, the next in April. After one year, they were receiving PV bonus checks that grossed $10,000 a month; after two years, that amount was over $24,000.

Most of that early distributor group the Behnkes developed were farmers. When they became Direct Distributors, they had a banquet to celebrate, and of the 200 distributors who attended, about 150 of them were farmers. Of that original group of four couples, all farming neighbors, who began with the Behnkes, two couples (the Benekes and the Wilkenses) are Diamonds today; the other two are Emerald and Pearl. All four couples gained financial independence from business; all four left their farms; all four moved to Kansas City. How you gonna keep 'em down on the farm after they've seen the circles?

As the Behnke business has spread, the percentage of distributors with nonfarming backgrounds has grown to 80 percent or more. Besides the Behnkes and the Wilkenses, seven other distributorships within their group have reached the Diamond level, and none of the seven were farmers. The life-style of the Behnkes themselves is not at all a rural one in recent years. They hold season tickets to the Kansas City Royals baseball games. They fly their own plane, take ski vacations to Europe—on one occasion they stayed four months —own a condo in Vail and a 3,400 square-foot mountain "cabin" on a lake in southern Colorado. "I didn't have any particular desire to leave the farm," Mel says, "and I could go back tomorrow if I wanted to. But now I do have that option, and that's what's exciting to Bea and me."

First Mel Behnke was a farmer.

Then he was a gentleman farmer.

Now he's just a gentleman.

He wouldn't have it any other way.

21 Two to Tango

FOR MOST PEOPLE, an Amway distributorship begins in the home. Small meetings are held there; products are kept there; the phone calls flow to and from there. And when two people—or more—occupy that hallowed space called "home," the decision to join Amway involves both husband and wife. A meeting of the minds is required. Sometimes the minds do not meet, at least not immediately.

It would be convenient if every husband-wife team who saw the Plan gained the same opinion of it. That often happens: they both like it and get in, or they both reject it and stay out. A neat conclusion, in either case. But what if one of them feels strongly that Amway is for them, and the other feels strongly that it is not? Well, of course, that *does* happen. For example. . . .

Meet the Puryears. Fine young couple from

Spokane, Washington, Ron and Georgia Lee Puryear. They grew up in a small Idaho town, were high-school sweethearts who married and went away to seek their fortunes, convinced that hard work and sacrifice would bring them their fair share of the Good Life. They worked Ron's way through college with lots of small jobs, not minding the privation because they were convinced it was temporary. At the end of it all, they thought, would come a job as an accountant and the comfortable middle-class life to go with it.

It didn't work out that way. After college came the job, but with the job quickly came disillusionment. "It took me about a week to figure out that you don't put bread and butter on the table with a title," Ron says. He soon found himself in the familiar position of the man who has a good job, doing what he is trained to do, but bringing home a paycheck too small to support his family. So Georgia Lee went to work at the best job she could find, which was as a waitress at a local Denny's restaurant.

Life was not much fun for the Puryears. With both incomes, they were paying the bills, but just barely and at the cost of being apart most of the time. Ron worked a regular nine-to-five day as an accountant. Georgia Lee worked from five to midnight, plus weekends, as a waitress. They passed, coming and going, in the driveway and took turns being with their two baby boys. Ron would wait up after midnight for her to return home each night, and they would have a few minutes together to visit and count the change Georgia Lee brought home in customers' tips, before falling into bed exhausted. It wasn't much of a life.

That was 1972. The Puryears got a phone call that winter from Jim and Sharon Elliott, friends they had met in the Pasco, Washington, area, a few years earlier. The Elliotts said they had something to tell the Puryears and would drive to Spokane for a weekend visit. "We hadn't seen them in four years," Ron remembers. "I couldn't believe they would come that far in the dead of winter, just to share some sort of business deal with me." But come they did, a five and a half hour drive in a Volkswagen, with their three preschool kids in the back. When they arrived, Jim showed Ron the circles, and Ron lit up like a Christmas tree. "I was excited! I could see immediately that this was for me. I couldn't wait for Georgia Lee to get home from work to see it."

She walked in that night, tired from eight hours on her feet, waiting tables, to find the three coconspirators sitting around the table, talking wildly about yachts and Cadillacs and trips to Hawaii; she could barely contain her anger enough to be civil to her guests. She listened to a quick explanation of the Plan, excused herself, and went to bed, leaving them where they sat.

"She was kind of rude," Ron says.

"I was disgusted and angry," she says.

"I think she went to bed mad," Ron says.

"I went to bed mad," she says.

But not Ron. He was too fascinated by this new

deal to sleep, so he and Jim sat up until 6:00 A.M. talking about Amway. "I realized he was showing me a second chance in life," Ron explains. "Let's face it, I wasn't cutting the mustard as the number-one breadwinner in my family. I was sick and tired of being broke. I married my wife to be with her, and we were separated sixteen hours a day. You've heard about a life of quiet desperation? Well, that's where I was. Jim really painted a dream for me that night. It seems funny, looking back. Here he was, as broke as me, driving a VW, and we were talking about financial independence and going to Hawaii! It was the most positive conversation I'd had in ten years."

So Mr. Puryear was ready to try it, but there was still Mrs. Puryear to deal with. She tells her side: "When I got up the next morning, I could see a different look in Ron's eyes. It scared me. I was afraid he was going to expect me to sell soap door to door all day and then wait tables at night. And I was already tired and busy. I gave him ten thousand logical reasons why we couldn't build this business."

So Ron did it alone, those first few months. "Okay," he told her, "if you won't do it with me, at least don't hold me back." He would do the retailing. He would do the prospecting. All she had to do was serve the coffee and not interfere. "When I have prospects at the house," said Ron, "all I ask is for you to have a dress on and a smile on your face."

"But I don't have a dress," said Georgia Lee.

"Go buy one," said Ron.

And on that note began what would become one of the most successful distributorships in the Northwest. Ron made his first sale—"a pair of pantyhose to an older woman down the street." He sold to housewives who knew more about household products than he could imagine. "Sure, I was scared," he admits. "But I got lots of experience and lots of customers." He tried to sponsor and had almost no success at first—nineteen straight refusals when he showed the Plan. But he kept trying, and when Georgia Lee saw that he wouldn't quit, when she was convinced that he was truly committed to it, she joined him.

It was not easy. Somehow she did not mind waiting tables in a restaurant, but was traumatized by the idea of selling a box of soap to a friend. Her first challenge was to show products to a neighbor whose backyard joined theirs, separated by a low fence. Ron walked with her out the back door and across the yard, trying to lend moral support. He lifted her across the fence, into the neighbor's yard. She climbed back over. "Ron, I can't do it," she whispered in the dark. "Sure you can," he replied and lifted her back over the fence. Again she climbed back into the security of her own yard. Again he reassured her and guided her over the fence. And this time she walked across the yard to her neighbor's back door, knocked, and went in.

In that first sales experience, as in so many things, the fear was much worse than the reality. By the time Georgia Lee came back home that night, she was as gung ho as her husband. "I got excited. Somehow, I really got excited. I saw I could do this thing, and I've been one hundred percent involved ever since."

With both members of the Puryear team sharing the project, the business grew faster. They became Direct Distributors fifteen months after Ron had first joined, and Georgia Lee left her waitressing job. But it was only after Ron began to dream of his own early "retirement" that they attacked the business with maximum effort. "Once I caught the glimpse of freedom, it consumed me. It was something we wanted badly, and we knew the key was work. We filled our calendar for the next two years; we worked as hard as we could, and after that two years, at the age of thirty-five, I retired, and I've never again worked for another man."

The Puryears are now Double Diamonds, and their sponsors, the Elliotts, are Diamond Directs. On the subject of Amway, quite naturally, all four of them are true believers, and Georgia Lee, the reluctant one in the beginning, is just maybe the truest believer of them all.

22 "Wait for Me; I'm Your Leader!"

SOMETIMES it works the other way.

In some partnerships, the original impetus toward Amway success comes from the wife, the husband coming aboard later.

Take the Trozeras, for example. Tom and Joy Trozera are Double Diamonds in California. In 1968, they were a fairly typical professional couple, with the basic upper-middle-class suburban life-style. He was an engineer with a Ph.D. in metallurgy from the University of California's Berkeley campus. The son of Sicilian immigrants, Trozera earned a reputation for himself as a scholar. After twelve years at Berkeley and eight years doing basic research, he had started his own electronics business, had published many technical articles and was widely regarded as being at the top of his area in the scientific community.

Still, all was not sweetness and light in the

Trozera household. While Tom was making a name for himself in the laboratory, Joy was at home quietly going nuts. "You've heard the phrase 'publish or perish?' " she asks. "Well, in our case Tom was publishing, and I was perishing. While he was in the lab all the time, I was going bananas!" (Nuts or bananas, it makes little difference.) So she went to work as an executive secretary, for personal fulfillment, and to help subsidize a forthcoming ski trip to Austria. As so often happens, the Trozera family expenses soon expanded to match the income. More income, more outgo. It didn't take long for the double paycheck to be an absolute necessity just to keep up with inflation. The high standard of southern California living requires lots of money, especially with the Trozeras' taste for such expensive diversions as skiing and European travel. As long as Joy was working, there was enough money to do most of it but as her sons got older, work became more and more burdensome. She began to want her freedom from the job.

"At first I enjoyed working," she says. "But after I had worked about six years and my boys got to be ten and twelve years old, I began to feel that I had missed a large part of their lives. I began looking for an alternative." After she and Tom were shown the Amway Plan, she eventually came to see it as a way to continue her income without tromping off to the office every morning. She decided to give it a try.

But not Tom. When Joy became a distributor,

he was so uninterested that he even declined the formality of signing the application form with her. Not that he was aggressively negative; he simply saw it as something for *her* to do. He couldn't relate to its being for himself. So Joy began alone, at first only using the products, then sponsoring new distributorships. She still remembers the first profitable month—they spent the bonus money on a ski trip to Utah—and the month after that one—they spent *that* bonus money skiing at Squaw Valley! Tom began to become more interested in Amway as a thing they could do together. The private business venture he had begun was doing poorly, and as it looked worse and worse, the Amway potential looked better and better. The other business finally collapsed entirely. "It was a glorious failure," recalls the candid Dr. Trozera. "And looking back, I'm glad now that it failed so completely. If it had had even the slightest iota of success, I don't think I would ever have looked seriously at Amway. But I was losing money hand over fist, almost two thousand dollars a month, and the Amway concept started to look more attractive."

When the Trozera Amway business became a joint effort, the impact was immediate. As in the earlier example of the Puryears, the combination of both partners pulling together worked miracles. Double the partnership, it seems, and you quadruple the results—or even better. It is a case in which one plus one does not make two, but five or ten or twenty. Within eight months, Joy's secretarial income had been matched by their business, and she "bought her freedom," as they described it. They became Direct Distributors within a year of signing up; and within sixteen months Tom had made the decision to leave his corporate vice-presidency. "I got a check that month for four thousand five hundred and sixty-eight dollars, and ninety-one cents," he remembers. "I can still see that check in glowing neon. I knew I was ready to buy *my* freedom." And he did just that.

Now Trozera is free to do research as he wishes and also has a private consulting practice. "Now I have the flexibility to consult when, where, and with whom I choose," he says, "because Amway makes me financially independent. So I enjoy my profession, on my terms. To me, this combination is the best of all possible worlds!"

Four thousand miles to the west of San Diego, across the Pacific, another couple were experiencing a similar introduction to the freedoms that Amway can bring. Like Tom Trozera, Howard Miura was an engineer who became an Amway distributor as a result of his wife's example—plus a little gentle nudging. The Miuras live in Honolulu, where Betty Lou was a schoolteacher with a family. Her children were five and seven years old, and she describes their pre-Amway life as "a comfortable rut." With their two paychecks, they didn't lack for any of the basic middle-class comforts, but there was very little left over at the end of the month. They were a rather average family;

they watched television every night; they played tennis every Saturday; they had just moved into a new home.

A fellow schoolteacher of Betty Lou's invited them to a business meeting one night, and she promised she and Howard would attend. Howard didn't want to go; the meeting fell on the same night as the Rainbow Classic, an important college basketball tournament in Honolulu, and he was annoyed that Betty Lou would drag him to a business meeting when he preferred to see a basketball game. She persuaded him to go with her, but only amid great grumbling and moaning, and he predictably paid little attention to the speaker when he got there. "I was there physically, that's all," he explains. "Mentally I was at the Rainbow Classic. I sat through that meeting and didn't hear or understand a thing."

No matter. Betty Lou was hearing. Betty Lou was thinking. Betty Lou was thinking she *liked* what she was hearing. Two days later, Betty Lou was signing up.

"At first I was unable to see myself selling," she says. "But I felt I could do it if I had to, and I was surprised, once I began, at how easy it was. The products were so good and I gave such good service to my customers that after a while they would literally call *me* to ask to buy products!" Howard joined Betty Lou immediately, to lend his support, and as the business grew he became more and more involved. Within just over a year, they had gone Direct, and today are Diamonds and the leaders of

Hawaii's largest distributor organization.

The Amway experience shook the Miuras out of that "comfortable rut." Betty Lou has long since resigned from her teaching job to become a full-time wife and mother. They take their children skiing on the mainland every winter. They have visited Japan on an Amway-sponsored speaking tour and spent time with old friends and relatives in Tokyo, Kyoto, and Osaka. "Of all the material payoffs from Amway," Betty Lou is asked, "what do you treasure most? Has Amway given you anything that might be called a dream come true?"

"A chance to see America the Beautiful!" she replies emphatically. "So many opportunities to see all this wonderful country of ours. My biggest dream, as a child growing up here on the islands, was to see America the Beautiful. I had seen so many pictures. And we have done that—traveled all over the United States—with our children. That was my lifelong dream! And that's what this business is, after all. This business is working for the things you really want, instead of settling for second best."

23 Sleeping Single in a Double Bed

FOR TENS OF THOUSANDS of Amway distributors, the whole matter of the husband-wife partnership is a nonissue. They are the singles—unmarried distributors who comprise an estimated 20 to 25 percent of the total distributor force. There may be as many as 200,000 of them in the United States, although no one knows for sure.

The option to stay single is being chosen by a higher percentage of America's young people, and those who marry tend toward earlier and more frequent divorces. As a result, the social structures in this country that formerly were oriented to the married couple are readjusting to accommodate this growing number of singles. Amway is no exception. What were once the rarest of all creatures —successful single Diamond Directs—are now becoming almost commonplace.

Stuart Menn is one of them. Born and educated in New York City, Menn now lives in southern California. He is forty-four years old and looks younger; he has never lost his Bronx accent, despite living all over the United States' map. He has never been married. Menn is a one-man refutation of the misconceptions many people hold of the "typical" Amway distributor. The stereotype is that the Amway distributor is a married blue-collar worker who belongs to a conservative Christian church and lives in a small town. Menn is a Jewish medical doctor, unmarried, from New York City and San Diego.

Menn's father, who is seventy-six years old, immigrated as a teenager, arriving in Manhattan's Lower East Side in 1912. Stuart grew up in the Bronx, always precocious and ambitious, and stayed in New York City through college and medical school at New York University. He developed an interest in pulmonary medicine and the emerging field called "aerospace medicine" and spent his fourth year of med school at the School of Aerospace Medicine in San Antonio, Texas. That decision would affect his entire career as a physician and ultimately lead him into Amway.

Menn finished his M.D.; went to Burlington, Vermont, for an internship; then to Pittsburgh for a residency in internal medicine. From there he went into the United States Air Force, where he spent two years doing research in carbon-dioxide-tolerance limits in sealed cabin environments. He returned to Vermont for a second year of residency, after which he went to Boston for a research fellowship at the famous Massachusetts General Hospital; finally he landed in San Diego to study and practice pulmonary medicine and set up an intensive-care unit at the Veterans Hospital there. (All this by the age of thirty-three; he didn't have *time* to get married!)

At this point in his career, the peripatetic Dr. Menn had a critical decision to make: to pursue a career in a private medical practice, or to stay in academic medicine. His heart was in academic medicine, but the money was in private practice. It is a common crossroad for bright young research-oriented physicians. To stay with what he most enjoyed meant giving up an additional income of roughly $50,000 a year that could be made in practice.

Lodged painfully on the horns of this dilemma, Stuart Menn remembered a business deal he had seen nearly three years earlier. Someone had shown him the Amway business during his last stint in San Antonio; he had signed an application, thrown his Amway kit into a closet somewhere, and promptly forgot it. Now, thirty months and many miles later, he remembered the name of his original sponsors, called them in Maryland, and started to build an Amway career that would ultimately match the level of success he had known in medicine.

"After the first three months," he says, "there

was no turning back. At that point it became a love affair between Amway and me." That was 1971, and for twelve years the Menn strategy has worked; his earnings from the Amway business have allowed him to do academic medicine without an overall loss of income. For a handsome bachelor in southern California, the combination of money to spend and time to spend it must surely mean having the best of both worlds.

On the other side of the continent, in another seaport city, Louise Williams represents a quite different type of single Diamond. She is small and pretty, with just a trace of the distinctive accent one hears so often in the Tidewater area of coastal Virginia.

Louise is a pioneer of sorts; she was the first single woman, working alone, to achieve Diamond status in the United States. (Earlier, two Ohio singles working as partners, Karen DeOreo and Paula Pritchard, had qualified as Diamonds, and a young Malaysian distributor, Tan Siew Lan, had become the first single woman to become a Diamond overseas.)

Louise has lived in Virginia's Tidewater area since early childhood. She was a student at William and Mary, graduating with a B.S. in physics in the late 1960s. From 1968 until 1981 she worked as an engineer in the aerospace industry, first for an independent contractor and for the last eight years for the National Aeronautics and Space

Administration (NASA). At NASA she worked as a flight simulation engineer, applied computers to acoustical research on helicopter noise, and most recently did aviation and space systems planning.

Successful as she was at NASA, Louise's Amway achievements brought her greater financial rewards and, eventually, more intangible benefits as well. "In Amway I found a company that was genuinely unconcerned with the fact that I was a woman," she says. "I don't like being treated better or worse, professionally, because I'm female. I just want to be accepted for what I produce. Period. That's the way it is in Amway. You get what you deserve. No more and no less." What she deserved apparently included a very large income, enough to put her into a Porsche and a Mercedes ("Well, I still keep the Mustang, too!") and a brick colonial home on a five-acre waterfront estate on the Poquoson River.

Louise enjoyed her work at NASA, and she enjoyed the life of a monied single woman, but in 1981 she gave up both. In December she married, to become Mrs. Paul Phillips. Earlier that year, in June, she had resigned her post at NASA to become a full-time Diamond. "I wanted to make sure I knew what I was doing," she says.

With Louise Williams' track record, one has little doubt that she did know. Her retirement from NASA was not an impulsive thing; it showed the lucid thought one expects from a top-notch engineer. The resignation letter, written four months ahead of her departure, shows the style of woman who knows exactly where she is going and why:

February 12, 1981

Dear George:

While in Hawaii on a well-earned vacation, I was able to spend considerable time evaluating my objectives and setting goals for the future. As a result, I now find myself doing something I never thought I would be doing. After considerable financial counseling, it has become apparent that the time has arrived for me to submit my resignation from government employment with NASA. My reasons for this decision are quite simple: first, due to the fact I was able to get into business for myself seven years ago, the income I have generated by doing so has far exceeded what I could possibly make with the government, allowing me to achieve many of my dreams and to help many worthwhile causes.

Therefore, for tax reasons and value of time, it does not make economic sense for me to continue working a job. Second, my parents raised me with the knowledge I could do anything I believed in, but I'd excel in whatever gave me the most enjoyment and room for creativity. Due to this, I feel my best assets and contributions lie in helping people achieve the real American dream: economic and personal freedom, a beautiful thing we can all possess.

I have found fulfillment and true happiness in being in business for myself and desire to spend more time sharing this opportunity. I have faith that our country can truly be free again if its citizens find a way to give their best and don't settle for just getting by.

In conclusion, although this is a letter of resignation, it is also a letter of appreciation. Except for one year of employment that instilled in me a desire to be elsewhere, my eight years with NASA have been very rewarding. I truly appreciate the cooperation of my supervisors as well as my co-workers. I have enjoyed the work and the responsibilities afforded me and am proud to have the opportunity to work at NASA.

With God's help, I look forward to a bright future for myself, for each of you, and for our country.

Sincerely,
Louise H. Williams

No question about it—*that* is leaving in style.

24 Loving It but Leaving It

LEAVING A JOB she genuinely enjoyed in favor of a full-time Amway career that she enjoys even more was perhaps the toughest decision Louise Williams Phillips has made since becoming a distributor. That dilemma is undoubtedly the most pleasant kind to face; it is a choice between the better of two positives, rather like selecting one of two appetizing desserts.

But even so, it is not an easy move to make. Indeed, the attractiveness of one's conventional job renders a decision to leave it more difficult, not less so. In making that decision, Louise Williams was aided by the knowledge that many more have faced it before her. As the Amway experience spreads to more and more individuals with high-income jobs, it will be more and more common for a Diamond, taking a last lingering look at his "regular" job, to decide to love it but leave it.

Jerry Webb did that. He was one of those mathematics whiz kids—the kind of guy you always hated to see enroll in your high school algebra class, because he always wrecked the grading curve. He was the kind of student who, when the teacher put an equation on the board, actually understood it.

Jerry and Sharyn, his wife, are from West Texas. They met at Lubbock Christian College, a small church-related school; married after two years there; then moved to Harding College, in Arkansas, to finish Jerry's undergraduate degree. From there the academic trail led them to the University of Texas, at Austin, where they settled for the years required for Jerry to complete his master's degree and Ph. D. in math.

The young couple lived thirty miles outside Austin, in the quaintly named town of Dripping Springs, Texas. (No kidding.) As Jerry moved closer to the Ph.D., however, it became increasingly important for him to be near the university computer, so they began looking for an apartment near the University of Texas campus. They found one and moved into it as the previous occupants moved out. That bit of timing was a lucky one for the Webbs, because the couple whose paths they crossed that day were Wayne and Sue Walker, who were Amway Direct distributors. What happened was inevitable. The mover-outers sponsored the mover-inners. What else?

That was in 1969, and their new Amway business didn't seem at the time to figure very prominently in the Webbs' future. Jerry completed his degree soon afterward and accepted an offer to stay at the University of Texas as an assistant professor of computer science and as research mathematician at the school's Center for Numerical Analysis. The experience of finishing school and entering the job market was something of a shocker for the Webbs. He was highly employable, with computers just coming into vogue as they were, but he was unprepared for near-total commitment of his time that prospective employers demanded. They offered good money, but expected him to give the corporation a virtually unlimited claim on him. He was unwilling to sell himself so totally to an oil company, however good the pay, so he stayed in the academic world.

Alma Mater called—the original alma mater for both Jerry and Sharyn: little Lubbock Christian College. To the deeply religious couple, the call to return there as head of the Mathematics Department was irresistible. "We really loved the school," Jerry says. "And it is our church school, so we couldn't say no." So back to Lubbock they went, this time to stay.

It was from Lubbock that the Webbs built one of Amway's most successful distributorships. They showed the Plan on a regular basis for the next several years. Their personal group volume grew much faster than their pin level did, up to $60,000 per month by 1976. At one time they had 1,300 people in their personal group and were still at the Ruby pin level. When they finally began to earn higher pin awards, the Webb distributorship was the talk of the Amway world. The speed with which they flew up the pin-level ladder was dazzling: Pearl in 1976, Emerald and Diamond in 1977, and Double and Triple Diamond and Crown Direct, all in 1978.

As their group of distributors began to multiply so rapidly, the contribution they were making at Lubbock Christian College grew less significant to them than the many other service opportunities that their Amway business created. Jerry stepped down as department head, then finally from the faculty altogether, to give his full attention to his "other" career.

Today they are Crown Ambassadors and more convinced than ever that they made the right move. "As we got bigger," Jerry says, "we thought about it a lot and finally concluded we just had to make sure our own priorities were straight and do what seemed best. We didn't get into Amway for the big money. We didn't even know it was available. Now we are making a lot of money, but we certainly are not chasing the bucks. There are lots of good things we can do with our money, and it's up to us to do them."

The Webbs back up their explanation with heavy financial support of causes they believe in. Among them: the establishment of a Richard DeVos Scholarship for young people studying at—where else?—Lubbock Christian College.

Darrel Rupe was never a high-school whiz kid,

but rarely met anyone who would outwork him on his way to becoming Dr. Rupe. For Darrel, that road was a long one, and he traveled it mostly on pluck and desire and the help of a good wife named DeLaine.

Darrel and DeLaine entered the professional world the hard way. They both grew up in Oklahoma, determined to earn a slice of the upper-middle-class pie. Darrel graduated from high school, worked for a few years as a fry cook, and finally made it to college. There he and DeLaine met. They helped each other through school, got married, and set their sights on optometry school. "We wanted one thing really badly," DeLaine remembers, "and that was for Darrel to be Dr. Darrel L. Rupe." He applied to optometry school at the University of Houston, and off they went, with a total bankroll of $400.

They made it simply because people like the Rupes always make it when they want something the way the Rupes did. Darrel collected soft-drink bottles and sold them. He sold his blood to a local blood bank for twenty dollars a pint, "just so we could eat." After four years of study and sacrifice, he graduated as a doctor of optometry. Dr. and Mrs. Rupe moved back to Oklahoma and, in 1971, opened a practice in Claremore, a small town about twenty-five miles from Tulsa. His practice grew steadily, and he thought he was finally settled down for a lifetime of optometry.

In February of 1975, a bowling buddy named Bob Crisp asked Darrel to come to his house to see a business deal. "I saw the Plan, asked questions for about an hour and a half, and decided I had found a way to make four hundred and eight dollars a month to buy a new bass-fishing boat and pickup truck I wanted. I went home and talked to DeLaine about it." DeLaine said no; Darrel said yes; so they got in. The first month their PV bonus check was $3.20. One year later they were Silver Producers and in to stay. Four years later they were Diamond Directs.

Gradually, being Dr. and Mrs. Darrel L. Rupe, O.D., seemed less and less important to the young couple. Despite the sacrifices they had made to gain it, despite the promise it had always held for them, the status it represented—despite all that—the practice of optometry slipped downward on the Rupes' scale of priorities. It just didn't seem as valuable anymore. Darrel began to take a day or two off, first occasionally, then frequently. By the time they went Diamond, he was working only three days a week.

In the summer of 1978, Dr. Rupe decided to look for a way to leave his practice entirely. He finally sold it in the spring of 1979, kept coming to the office one day a week for a few months, to provide a gradual withdrawal, then at year's end retired altogether. He has not missed optometry, he says, and has no regrets about leaving it.

Darrel Rupe is one of those rare individuals who does not allow one good deal to obscure a better one. The same quiet drive and determination that got him through optometry school got him to Diamond. And the wife who supported his decision to pursue optometry was the same wife who supported his desire to leave it. When the time came, they walked away together, without a backward look.

Dr. Rupe sums it up, without a blink: "Optometry was a level I went through. I moved past it." The freedom to hold such an attitude, to express it, and to act on it, is truly an uncommon freedom.

25 The Forty-Hour Chore

UNFORTUNATELY, most working Americans would not describe their jobs as either enjoyable or rewarding. To the average breadwinner—blue collar or white—the job is just a job, a way to put bread on the table, a forty-hour chore between weekends.

One need not be a factory laborer to dislike his work. Even when the pay and presumed status of one's occupation are relatively high, a job frequently comes to be an irksome grind. The wage earner or salaried employee copes with an unsympathetic boss, an inflexible clock-punching routine, and a feeling of going nowhere. The professional or business person avoids those irritations, but must contend with heavy overhead expenses, the demands of clients or patients, and the constant pressure of being in the office for the fifty- and sixty-hour weeks required to keep it all going.

In either case, the job is something less than a joy. Virtually millions of job-weary Americans across the whole gamut of occupations—bricklayers and briefcase-carriers alike—can relate to the desire to summarily dismiss their jobs. Sometimes even the person who doesn't knock his job is merely making the best of a bad situation; a more accurate gauge of his attitude comes when he sees a viable way to leave it. When that happens, one best not stand between the employee and the nearest open door. Some of the best stories in Amway are stories of acting out the fantasy of punching the clock for the last time.

Chuck and Charlene Harrison have had that experience. They are from Greensboro, North Carolina, an upwardly mobile black couple in their mid-thirties. Chuck grew up with an unusually close relationship with his father and talks of him quietly, almost tenderly, with deep emotion: "My father had six sons, and I was the baby. We were close, he and I, very close. My father worked two jobs all his life. You could see the strain on him. He literally worked himself to death. He had all us boys to raise; we were a very religious family; and I believe he worked himself to death. He got sick and weak, and he would say to me, 'Son, I'm just tired.' That was the closest he ever came to complaining. 'Son, I'm just tired.' And he died."

Like father, like son. When Chuck and Charlene were married and began a family, he turned from the bachelor life ("I loved to dance and sing and follow the bands") to the responsibilities of providing for his own family and did so with a vengeance. He started work in a furniture factory, then moved to a job in a textile mill. Charlene worked in the post office and hurried home to care for their two sons. Chuck would work all night at the mill—occasionally working a second-shift job spray painting—then would leave there to work as a janitor cleaning office buildings. The bills were being paid, and the kids were being fed, but Chuck and Charlene were seeing very little of each other. "We were both working hard," Charlene says, "but we got farther and farther apart. We got to where we couldn't communicate. We really were not satisfied with our lives at that time."

Their chance to break out came in 1975. George and Ruth Halsey, neighbors whom the Harrisons knew socially, asked one day if they would be interested in something that could make them $30,000 a year. The Halseys were Amway distributors, not yet Directs themselves, but full of confidence that the Plan would work both for them and for the Harrisons. "They came at the right time," Chuck says. "My life was a rat race. I wanted to change things." Charlene had tunnel vision; she had a single goal in mind: "I had dreams of leaving that post office!" So the Harrisons added the Amway business to their already exhausting schedule.

It was hard work. "We ate a lot of hot dogs and hamburgers to build this business," Chuck recalls. "I got off at three-thirty every afternoon, before Charlene; I'd fix something for supper; we would sit down to eat, take a quick shower, and *go!*"

Their sponsors soon broke Direct, and the next
month the Harrisons followed them. "Whenever
we got discouraged, the Halseys kept telling us
they believed in us. They urged us not to quit, saying that it would come together, and we believed
them. There were times when we would drive six or
seven hours to show the circles, and get there to a
no-show. There were times when Chuck would be
driving back from a meeting and have to pull off
the road for a five-minute sleep before going on.
He would get home, then get up and be at work the
next morning, come home that afternoon, take a
shower, get out easel and board, and go to show
the Plan again. We didn't mind, because we knew
that was our freedom!"

It was. The Harrisons built a solid business,
qualified as Emeralds less than three years after
getting in, and became Diamonds two years later.
The Halseys have gone all the way to Triple
Diamond and are members of the elite Executive
Diamond Council. Both couples have all the trim-
mings: big homes, Cadillacs and Mercedes (and a
Rolls Royce for the Halseys), foreign travel
("We've been more places in four years in this
business than in thirty-four years before"), and expensive clothes and jewelry. But none of that is as
sweet to the Harrisons as the big payoff: freedom
from their jobs.

Charlene first: "I worked at the post office for
eleven and a half years. That last day was the most
exciting day of my life. I had four hours left to

work. I walked down to the post office on the last day, and I stood there at my sorting machine and watched that clock. Right at twelve noon, I cut my machine off, I went to that clock, and I punched out for the last time. I walked straight out of that post office, and I never looked back! Never! This business had made me free from that rut job!''

Then it was Chuck's turn: he made his last day at the mill a memorable one; he showed up for work—late—at 10:00 A.M., wearing a brand new suit and a pair of white shoes. ''It was the first time in nine years at that place that anybody had ever seen me in a suit!'' He made the rounds, told everyone good-bye, and walked out to his freedom.

The drive to be free from an oppressive job is an uncommonly powerful one. Reaching out for something different requires a certain amount of audacity, a declaration to one's co-workers that one has had enough of that life, that one is willing to risk a bit of himself in order to move toward something better.

It is not surprising that the effort to become free so often ends with a flourish, some symbol that one era of a person's life is ending and a new one is beginning. For Jim Martin, a veterinarian in Kentucky who became a Diamond, that symbol meant sending out formal, engraved retirement announcements when he was quitting his practice to go full-time. To Bob Smiley, a Diamond who left government service in Washington, D.C., it included a public ceremony in which he buried his alarm clock. For Dick Hopper, an intense young delivery-truck driver in Pryor, Oklahoma, the occasion was marked even more elaborately.

Hopper was a native Californian who, with his wife, Dawn, and two young children, moved to Oklahoma in search of work. He found plenty of work, but not much money. He had already run through a string of jobs: a mud mixer on a construction crew, stock boy in a trading-stamp store, pumping gas on the night shift at a filling station. The first year of his marriage, he had worked at five jobs, collected five W-2 forms at the end of the year, and had grossed only $5,200 for the year. At the time the Hoppers began their Amway business, he wasn't doing much better than that. He drove a delivery truck for a soft-drink bottler and was paid nine and a half cents for every case he delivered. That adds up slowly.

The Hoppers found Amway well suited to their hard-working style and put together a big business in near-record time. His second year in Amway he earned $57,000 from his distributorship and in the same period made $12,413 driving the soft-drink truck. So when he went to the warehouse for his final day, he showed his Oklahoma friends a bit of California flair. He wore a tuxedo to work that day, read a retirement letter to his pop-truck buddies as his sponsor filmed the event with a home-movie camera. A marching band showed up to add a festive note to the occasion, playing "Taps" as he left the premises for the last time.

Anthropologists insist that man uses special symbolic occasions to mark the important events in life, such as weddings, baptisms, and bar mitzvahs. These ceremonies, they say, serve to underscore the passing from one stage of life to another.

Dick Hopper, who has never met a real life anthropologist, figured that out all by himself.

26 The Amway "Type"

TRYING TO UNDERSTAND *why* the Amway system works invariably leads to a discussion of temperament, of personality type. There is a notion that those who succeed in Amway must fit some particular profile of personal traits. "What *kind* of person can do this business?" one is asked. If a good astronaut must be cool and unflappable, an accountant must be meticulous and careful, and a good trial lawyer must be persuasive and articulate, what must a good Amway distributor be?

Rent the largest computer available, stuff it with the life histories of all the Amway Diamonds, ask it that question, and what you will likely get is not a personality profile but a blown fuse and a repair bill for the computer.

The answer does not exist. Are good Amway distributors outgoing and extroverted? Or are they reserved and quiet? Are they well-organized, detail-oriented types? Or are they spontaneous on-the-run planners? Do they analyze, or do they operate by instinct? Is the Amway "type" an individual with flair and pizzazz who takes naturally to the spotlight and the speaker's stage, or is the Amway type a quietly determined individual who moves steadily toward his goals with a minimum of display?

The answer to all these questions is yes.

Bob Vest and Keith Belknap, for example. Each is the Amway type. Each is characteristic of a particular approach to this unusual business, and each approach has worked very well. The Vest style and the Belknap style seem to fit the demands of the Amway experience perfectly, and in each case a solid distributorship has been built past the Diamond level. But the Vest and Belknap styles could never be stuffed into the same pigeonhole; they are as different as fire and ice; they are personality types with almost nothing in common, except that each is obviously the perfect type for Amway.

Keith Belknap has one of the most spectacular records of fast growth in Amway history and a spectacular personal style to match it. He is made up of equal parts of self-confidence, adrenaline, and onstage charm. He is colorful and provocative; he virtually throbs with energy and ambition. "I *am* a strong leader," he declares. "I make no apologies for it. When you look at me; you're looking at a winner." His wife, Jimmie, says he proposed marriage to her on their first date. That sounds completely in character for Belknap, who has always known what he wants and has gone after it. "My grandfather took one look at Keith," Jimmie remembers, "and told me if I married him, I would never be broke!"

Well, she married him, twenty-eight years ago, and she is definitely not broke today. (Chalk up one for grandfather.)

The Belknaps are Triple Diamonds. They were sponsored into Amway in late 1977 and by July of 1979 had already qualified as Double Diamonds. They live in Tulsa, Oklahoma, and for years traveled with their children—Keith, Jr., and Kim—as gospel singers. "We sang all over the United States," Jimmie says. "Big crowds, little crowds—we sang every night. We learned it didn't matter how you felt, you still went out there and sang." Gospel music barely made a living for the Belknaps, so Keith saved enough money to begin developing commercial real estate. He parlayed an initial investment of $8,000 into a substantial net worth and was expanding his development activities at the time he saw the Amway Plan.

He tells it: "A guy who leased office space from me told me he had heard something that 'sounded pretty good,' so we went together to see it. At first I turned it down because I couldn't see starting at the bottom. We talked about it around our house for a few days, decided not to do it, and made a pact never to mention Amway again. But it ate at me. It wouldn't let me go. One day Kim and I were sitting in a restaurant. It was down at Buns 'n'

Burgers in Tulsa. We started dreaming. We started
playing 'what if?' We started talking about all the
things we'd like to do and the places we'd like to
go, and we got excited about the possibilities that
could be out there in Amway.

"That was the turning point. After that I got in
touch with the guy who had tried to sponsor me; I
called him at one o'clock in the morning, and said,
'Bring me a sales kit!' He did, and we were in."
Soon after that Buns 'n' Burgers afternoon, Keith
and Kim drove to California to sponsor an old
friend, and out of that trip came another Diamond
distributorship. The Belknaps acknowledge that
they have worked virtually nonstop since coming
into the business. "Sure, it takes work," he says.
"This is like anything else; it's there for those who
want it. Amway is not for lazy people. It's not for
losers. But for the people who want something and
are ready to work for it, it's absolutely the best
business there is!"

The entire Belknap family shows a talent for
Amway leadership. Keith Jr. and his wife Ann
Marie are Emeralds today; Kim and her husband Bill Nash recently qualified as Diamonds.
Jimmie's parents, and an uncle and aunt, have also
come into the business and built to the Diamond
level.

Keith Belknap, for all his personal charisma, is
unwilling to attribute his success to that flamboyant style. Could it be possible, he is asked, that a
dynamic style like his is necessary to build a big
distributorship? "Absolutely not!" he responds.

"It just happens that I have the kind of personality I have, but you don't have to be great on stage to build this business. When I got into Amway, for the first time in my life I was able to be myself. But people are different. Somebody can get into Amway with about as much charisma as a carburetor and go right to Diamond. He can live off someone else's charisma, if he has to, until his own develops."

What, then, is the thing that makes it work? If not personal charisma, what is it? It is a question for which he has an immediate answer: "Inner drive," he says. "I had that inner drive. That's what it takes."

No one who knows Bob Vest has ever doubted that he has "that inner drive," though packaged in a more restrained personal style than Belknap's. He is a former engineer, with all the patterns of the profession: logical, deliberate, well reasoned, and absolutely reliable. And just as Belknap brought the influence of the gospel-music stage to his Amway career, so Vest brought to his Amway business all the training of an engineering career—and with the same success.

Bob and Linda Vest live in Cincinnati; they are now Double Diamonds, and Bob is a member of the board of the Amway Distributors Association. In Amway circles, his name is virtually synonymous with integrity and solid leadership. He had been an engineer, living by the slide rule and the drawing board, for over ten years when he saw the business. He made a good salary and enjoyed his work, but looked ahead ten and fifteen years in his profession and could see little chance of ever being substantially ahead of where he was. He was frustrated by that lack of potential and by the lack of freedom in his job, so when he heard the Amway Plan explained, he was tempted to try it.

But there was that question of style. *Am I the right type of person for Amway?* he wondered. "We were so afraid we might not be able to do it," Linda recalls, "because we just didn't know if we would be successful." But Bob was determined to try it anyway. Eventually, after he had worked alone for a few months, Linda also got involved, and the distributorship grew. Not on charisma, but on that inner drive.

"We got there by setting goals and by sheer determination," Bob says. "Any engineer knows how to set goals. I took a sheet of graph paper, laid it out, estimated the number of people needed to have a Direct distributorship, plotted it out over three months, and treated it like any systems planning problem." He kept graphs with multicolored lines: graphs of projected volume, actual volume, graphs of distributor counts, and various other indicators of progress. Looking back, he admits that all those logical charts and projections were not very useful; that method was simply the way he was trained to attack a job. The point is that he *did* attack it. The engineering approach gradually gave way to a more spontaneous one. "Goals that are too logical are too low," he says. "I learned to dream bigger."

A profitable Double Diamondship can support very big dreams, the Vests have discovered. Bob has long since left his engineering job, and with Linda and his three daughters, enjoys a life-style that his former career could never have brought them. He is without question the Amway type, as is Belknap. Slide rules and graphs prepared him well for his Amway success, as microphones and music prepared Belknap for his.

For Vest, as for Belknap, the inner drive is the critical variable. Everything else is simply a matter of style.

27 A Family Affair

How does an Amway experience affect the family?

That question is an inevitable one for conscientious parents who are engaged in—or even who are considering—an Amway distributorship. Clearly, Amway works best when the distributor works hardest. The stories of dramatic success that make up the Amway legend always occur as a result of a major commitment of time and attention to the task of building the business. When the distributors involved are parents of young children and the place of business is the home, the effect of the experience on family life is an obvious concern.

Is the overall impact of the Amway connection good or bad for the children of successful distributors?

Ask Tim and Sherri Bryan. They are among the

most successful Amway leaders in northern New
England. Both are in their mid-thirties and have
been in the business eleven years, so their preteen
children have lived in an Amway home virtually all
their lives. They are from Portland, Maine, where
Tim was an elementary-school teacher and Sherri
was a legal secretary before Amway.

They were sponsored by a relative who lived in
New Jersey, and in the early days of their distributorship, drove three hours for their regular product pickup. Maine was not the most fertile field
for Amway in the early 1970s, and they admit that
building a business then was tough. Tim spent
many days and nights on the road, away from his
family, because that was what the business required from him. "Was it a bad bargain in terms
of the family," he is asked? "Was it a mistake to
take that time away from the family?"

"No way!" he responds. "Not at all! Look, I
was making seven thousand six hundred dollars a
year as a schoolteacher. Sherri was working full
time. We never had any time *or* money! When
you're working to get out of that kind of life,
you're doing yourself and your wife and your kids
a favor. You bet it's worth it! What we have now
lets us be with our kids as we never could have
without Amway."

The Bryans also emphasize the nonfinancial
benefits of an Amway life for their children. "It
was in this business that I really learned how to
love," Tim says. "I've had people in Amway who
showed me for the first time in my life what love

really was. I've had people help me when there was nothing in it for them at all, financially. And that has made me a better man and a better father. It rubs off on the kids. Amway families have a love that they see on a day-by-day experience, and that's hard to find."

Sherri feels strongly that her children, raised in the Amway experience, wouldn't have it any other way. "My kids really feel pride in Amway," she says. "I remember when Dean, our son, saw his daddy draw the circles for the first time; he was so impressed with that! And a few days later we came in and he was sitting there drawing the circles for the baby-sitter! My kids have learned so much pride and so much love from this business. The way the world is today, I would be scared to raise my kids without this business and without the faith we have learned from Amway."

The Bryans' attitude characterizes that of many Amway parents. Not just the money, but the attitudes kids learn, constitute important payoffs from their business experience.

Kids apparently *do* learn positive attitudes from being around the Amway environment. Few families would know more about that than the Delisle family of California—seventeen family members in the business, nine of whom are full-time, including a Crown Ambassadorship and Triple and Double Diamondships. One of the Delisle grandchildren, the six-year-old daughter of

Dennis and Sharon, used the word *goal* at school one day and was asked what the word meant. "Well," she pondered, "a goal is where, whatever you want, you write it down and put it on the refrigerator door, and it always comes true!"

Also included among those positive attitudes is a healthy respect for parents, as Amway children watch dad and mom make sacrifices to provide a better life.

"I am my two daughters' hero," says Tennessee Diamond Jim Agard. "I've earned that. I can't think of anything better a man could get from this business than the admiration of his kids, because they've seen him pay a price for them. One of my daughters was assigned to write a paper in school about her hero, and she wrote it about me. I'll admit that when I read it, I couldn't hold back the tears! Her feeling that way means more to me than the money!"

Eight-year-old Scottie Michael, son of Ohio Diamonds Scott and M. J. Michael, expressed his hero worship in a more childish way. He had done well in school and was due a reward for his efforts. "What would you like for a reward?" his mother asked. "I'd like to have my name changed," he replied. "I want to be called Scott Michael, just like my dad!"

Home-based entrepreneurs who achieve great success have an excellent opportunity to elicit that kind of healthy admiration from their children, and that seems a potent part of family life in Amway. "I would rather my kids believe Abraham Lincoln was a horse thief than believe their dad is not a winner!" one Diamond declared.

For many full-time Amway parents, the major attraction of the business is the promise of more time with their children.

Jerry and Peggy Boggus are Georgia Diamonds who typify the many bright young parents who see Amway primarily as a family business. Jerry, an army captain at Fort Bragg, was having second thoughts about his military career when he saw the Plan. "Out of the last four years, I had spent two of them away from my family," he says. "I hated that. I'm a family man; I hate to be away from them. I could almost be content never to go anywhere, so long as I was with my family. But my job was interfering with that."

To remedy that problem, Jerry and Peggy became Amway distributors. In the beginning, they admit, the business took them away more than it kept them home. "When we got in," Peggy tells, "my children were four, three, and one and one-half years old. There was no way they could understand what we were doing at the time. They didn't like being left. If we depended on their positive response to the business at that time, we wouldn't be in Amway today. But we have talked to them about it and shared it with them as they have grown older, and now they are the biggest dreamers in the family! There were times when they didn't understand, but they sure love the Amway life-style now!'' The *now* includes a sprawling country estate near Augusta, with horses for all three children, who are now fourteen, thirteen and eleven.

John Perkins, a Diamond in Massachusetts, came into Amway with an attitude much like that of Jerry Boggus. "My own father worked all the time," he explains. "He never took a vacation. He never had any time with the kids. I was seventeen years old when he died and was just getting to know him. So that became my biggest motivation, to build this business so I could be with my kids. I've been a full-time father since 1973. That's reason enough for me to do this thing!''

Sometimes that time spent together comes in glamorous places, another advantage for families Amway parents frequently mention. "We believe that the family that travels together stays together," a father put it recently. No one believes that more strongly than the Payne family. Tom and Carolyn are Triple Diamonds from Alabama. Sons Scott (fifteen) and Lee (thirteen) can barely remember when Amway was not an important part of their lives. When one evaluates the impact of an intensive Amway involvement on children, the best argument for the business is kids like Scott and Lee.

Each is bright and healthy, highly motivated, every inch the Southern gentlemen. They are not pampered rich kids, though they enjoy a ski condo in Colorado, a summer home in the north Georgia mountains, vacations in Europe, and the best of everything that money can buy. They are what was once called "respectful" kids—one can see they were certainly not neglected in the process of building a big business. One senses that the Payne sons, like so many Amway children, do not take for granted what they have because they have *seen* the work required to produce it. They can hardly avoid learning that rewards follow performance, because the work of Amway, unlike that of dentistry or law or whatever, goes on all around them.

There is in the Payne home that uncommon bond among family members which is seen repeatedly in the homes of leading Amway distributors. It is perhaps the most difficult atmosphere to create in any modern home in the go-go 1980s: an atmosphere of mutual effort, mutual goals, mutual interests.

Another Amway father put it this way: "Amway means to me the freedom to have a home that's really a home, with a family that is there full-time, all of us working together and reaping the rewards together. We don't have a situation anymore where I have my life, and my wife has hers, and the kids have theirs, and we don't know what the others are doing. We have a family now, a real family, and the life we have in Amway we can all share together."

That spells *family* in capital letters.

Epilogue

THERE ARE MANY FREEDOMS.

The best freedoms are the most elusive ones—the ones for which the greatest effort must be made. Those are the freedoms of which Amway people most often talk: the freedom to be a full-time parent, freedom to share honest emotions unself-consciously, freedom to trust and be trusted, freedom to work where the heart and not just the paycheck leads, freedom to be a hero to one's kids.

There are more tangible freedoms, too, of which Amway distributors dream: freedom from the alarm clock, the commuter-bus schedule, the nine-to-five drudge; freedom to live in that better house, in that better neighborhood; freedom to take the kids along when they want to go; freedom to play golf at Pebble Beach instead of Peckerwood Municipal; freedom merely to pay the bills;

freedom not to worry about retirement.

These are truly uncommon freedoms. Most men and women wish for them, dream of them, but never find a way to have them. Amway's extraordinary momentum and energy comes from the conviction of its people that they have found a way to earn those freedoms. One distributor puts it this way: "The best thing I get from this business is the freedom to look in the mirror every morning and know that I am becoming the person I've always wanted to be!"

DR. ROBERT ANTHONY

__**THE ULTIMATE SECRETS OF TOTAL SELF-CONFIDENCE**__ 0-425-10170-3/$4.99
Join the successful people who have mastered the principles of Total Self-Confidence. Put all aspects of your life under your control.

__**DR. ROBERT ANTHONY'S MAGIC POWER OF SUPER PERSUASION**__ 0-425-10981-X/$3.99
Simple, but powerful. Strengthen your art of communication and be a top achiever!

__**50 GREAT IDEAS THAT CAN CHANGE YOUR LIFE**__ 0-425-10421-4/$4.50
Fifty concepts designed to make self-evaluation easier than ever.

__**DR. ROBERT ANTHONY'S ADVANCED FORMULA FOR TOTAL SUCCESS**__
0-425-10804-X/$4.50
Using simple step-by-step methods, turn your dreams into a reality of total success!

THE THINK BOOKS

In today's fast-paced, mixed-up world, Dr. Robert Anthony's THINK books offer solutions of hope, encouragement, and cheer. Every book contains 80 ideas, each on a separate perforated page—so you can easily tear out the ones you want to tack up or take with you!

__**THINK** 0-425-08747-6/$3.50

__**THINK AGAIN** 0-425-09572-X/$3.50

__**THINK ON** 0-425-11186-5/$3.50
